The AltaVista Search Revolution

Richard Seltzer
Deborah S. Ray
Eric J. Ray

Osborne **McGraw-Hill**

Berkeley   New York   St. Louis   San Francisco
Auckland   Bogotá   Hamburg   London   Madrid
Mexico City   Milan   Montreal   New Delhi   Panama City
Paris   São Paulo   Singapore   Sydney
Tokyo   Toronto

Osborne **McGraw-Hill**
2600 Tenth Street
Berkeley, California 94710
U.S.A.

For information on translations or book distributors outside the U.S.A., or to arrange bulk purchase discounts for sales promotions, premiums, or fundraisers, please contact Osborne/**McGraw-Hill** at the above address.

The AltaVista Search Revolution

1234567890 DOC 9987

ISBN 0-07-882235-1

Publisher	**Proofreader**
Brandon A. Nordin	Pat Mannion
Acquisitions Editor	**Indexer**
Megg Bonar	Valerie Robbins
Project Editor	**Computer Designer**
Claire Splan	Roberta Steele
Associate Project Editors	**Illustrator**
Cynthia Douglas	Richard Whitaker
Heidi Poulin	
	Quality Control Specialist
Editorial Assistant	Joe Scuderi
Gordon Hurd	
	Cover Design
Copy Editor	Ted Mader Associates
Gary Morris	

To my wife, Barbara, for her insights and limitless patience.

—Richard

About the Authors

Richard Seltzer is a marketing consultant in the Internet Business Group at Digital. He frequently speaks on Internet topics, acting as an advocate for full and more effective use of the Internet for business and education. In addition, Richard runs his own small publishing business on the Internet (The B&R Samizdat Express), and is the author of novels (*The Name of Hero*) and children's books (*The Lizard of Oz*). His electronic newsletter Internet-on-a-Disk has a readership of over 100,000, and his acclaimed Web site (**http://www.samizdat.com/**) is frequently cited as an important resource for education and the blind. A graduate of Yale ('69), he has a master's degree in comparative literature (Russian, French, and German) from the U. of Mass. He lives in Boston with his wife Barbara and four extraordinary children. He can be reached at **seltzer@samizdat.com** or **richard.seltzer@ljo.dec.com**.

Eric J. Ray and Deborah S. Ray, co-authors of *HTML for Dummies Quick Reference,* and *Dummies 101: HTML,* and other technical publications, own RayComm, Inc., a technical communications consulting firm.

Eric has been involved with the Internet for over four years and has made numerous presentations and published several papers about HTML and online information. His technical experience includes creating and maintaining the TECHWR-L listserv list as well as implementing and running Web servers. As a technical communicator, Eric has received numerous awards from the Society for Technical Communication, including a Director-Sponsor Award, as well as from previous employers for his contributions to technical communication projects.

Deborah, a technical communicator for the past three years, has been involved with the Internet for the past two. She has varied technical experience, including developing various computer and engineering documents as well as teaching technical writing to college students. Deborah is well accomplished in technical communication, having received awards from the Society for Technical Communication as well as previous employers for her accomplishments in the field.

Eric and Deborah can be reached at **ejray@raycomm.com** and **debray@raycomm.com**, respectively, or through their Web site at **http://www.raycomm.com/**.

1 Introduction to AltaVista Search 1

2 Getting Started with AltaVista Search 9

3 Advanced Search 37

4 Searching Usenet Newsgroups 59

5 Providing Information the AltaVista Way 83

6 Using the AltaVista Search A to Z Reference 107

7 The AltaVista Story 215

A The Top 1,000 Most Common Words on the World Wide Web . . 239

B A Sample of 1,000 Queries 255

C Frequency of Words Used in AltaVista Search Queries 263

Index 267

CONTENTS AT A GLANCE

1 Introduction to AltaVista Search 1

   ALTAVISTA SEARCH: THE REVOLUTION! 3

     AltaVista Search's Scope 3

     AltaVista Search's Speed 3

     AltaVista Search's Ease of Use 4

   SO, WHAT'S SO REVOLUTIONARY,
     ANYWAY? 4

     In the Beginning 4

     Then Came Information
       Search Problems 5

     Then Came a Few Solutions . . . (Sort of) 6

     Then Came AltaVista 7

     Welcome to the Revolution! 8

2 Getting Started with AltaVista Search 9

   ABOUT THE ALTAVISTA SEARCH HOME
     PAGE 10

     Your Navigation Choices 12

     About the Simple Search Form 13

     Making AltaVista Search Your Home Page 17

   DOING SIMPLE SEARCHES 18

     Simple Search with Standard Output 19

     Saving Results 20

   HONING YOUR SIMPLE SEARCH SKILLS 22

     Using Rare Words 23

     Using All Words That Might Matter 24

     Using Phrases When You Know the Exact
       Word Order 25

     Using Punctuation and Spaces 26

     Using Capitalization 26

     Using Accent Marks Where Applicable 27

     Making Character Substitutions 27

     Using Wildcards When You Aren't Sure of
       the Exact Word 28

     Searching According to Structural Elements 30

     Requiring Specific Words or Phrases 34

     Excluding Specific Words and Phrases 34

CONTENTS

Combining Elements in Your Searches 35
Inslude AltaVista Search in Your Home Page 35

3 Advanced Search **37**
Why Use Advanced Search? 39
ABOUT THE ADVANCED SEARCH PAGE 39
ABOUT THE ADVANCED SEARCH FORM 41
About Operators: and**, or, near,** and **not** **42**
Grouping Operators and Expressions 45
Parentheses, Math, and Other Technical Stuff 45
Troubleshooting Tips 47
Restricting Your Search by Date 48
Ranking within Advanced Search 50
About Counting Results 51
BRINGING IT ALL TOGETHER: A SAMPLE
ADVANCED SEARCH 52
What's the Difference? Comparing
Advanced Search with Simple Search 55

4 Searching Usenet Newsgroups **59**
About Newsgroups 61
HOW ALTAVISTA SEARCH IMPROVES
NEWSGROUPS 63
SEARCHING NEWSGROUPS 64
ABOUT NEWSGROUP SEARCH RESULTS 65
Word Count 66
Documents 67
Date 67
Group 67
Sender 67
Local (L) 67
Binary (B) 68
Subject 68
Page Numbers 68
Footer 69
NEWSGROUP SEARCH STRUCTURAL
ELEMENTS 69
from: 69

subject: 70

newsgroups: 71

summary: and keywords: 71

About Newsgroup Categories 71

FINE-TUNING SIMPLE USENET SEARCHES 73

How to Find Replies to Your Own Postings 73

Keeping your Newsgroup Postings from
Being Found 75

DOING AN ADVANCED SEARCH OF
USENET 76

Review of Advanced Operators 79

FINE-TUNING ADVANCED USENET
SEARCHES 80

5 Providing Information the AltaVista Way 83

HOW ALTAVISTA SEARCH WORKS FOR
WEB PAGES 85

How AltaVista Search Finds Sites 85

How AltaVista Search Indexes Sites 86

How AltaVista Search Ranks Sites 87

What AltaVista Search Does Not Index 89

Controlling How AltaVista Search Indexes
Your Site 91

HTML Document Title 92

Abstract 93

Dates 94

Keywords 94

EXCLUDING PAGES OR SITES FROM
ALTAVISTA SEARCH 96

Why Exclude? 97

How to Exclude Pages or Sites 98

DESIGNING YOUR SITE 98

USEFUL TECHNIQUES FOR WEBMASTERS 100

Keeping Private Information Private 100

Taking Inventory of Links 100

Keeping Up with Links to and from Your
Site 101

Fixing Broken Links...102

Overall Site Inventory 102

HOW ALTAVISTA SEARCH FINDS NEWS
ARTICLES 104

EXCLUDING NEWS ARTICLES FROM
ALTAVISTA SEARCH...104

Using AltaVista Search for Searches of
Your Site 105

6 **Using the AltaVista Search A to Z Reference** **107**

INFORMATION IN THE REFERENCE...108

A TO Z REFERENCE ORGANIZATION 109

WHY SHOULD I USE THE A TO Z
REFERENCE?...110

HOW SHOULD I USE THE A TO Z
REFERENCE?...110

A TO Z REFERENCE CONVENTIONS 111

7 **The AltaVista Story** **215**

SO, WHERE DID ALTAVISTA COME FROM?................................216

SETTING THE STAGE..217

DIGITAL ON RESEARCH 217

PIONEERING THE INTERNET 218

Building a Showcase 220

Scooter 221

Comments from the Inside: Philip Steffora.............................221

How Can It Work So Fast? 222

A Database or an Index?..223

How Does the Indexer Work? 224

Making It Happen..225

So What's an Alpha? Where's the Omega?...............................226

BUILDING THE PROTOTYPE 228

THE PITCH!..230

Piping Information into the Internet...230

The Internal Pilot 232

So What's in a Name? 232

THE LAUNCH!.. 234
    Comments from the Inside: Annie Warren.................................... 234
    The Birth of a New Business.. 235
EXTENDING SUCCESS 236
THE ALTAVISTA REVOLUTION
    CONTINUES … 237

A The Top 1,000 Most Common Words on the World Wide Web 239
    HOW TO SEARCH MOST EFFECTIVELY...................................... 240

B A Sample of 1,000 Queries 255

C Frequency of Words Used in AltaVista Search Queries.................... 263

Index.. 267

The creation of this book was a collaborative effort involving the help of many people.

First of all, we wish to thank Ilene Lang from AltaVista Internet Software for making this book possible. We also wish to thank: Kathleen Greenler, also from AltaVista Internet Software, for her hard work and dedication in pulling the project together and actually finishing it. Louis Monier, one of the researchers who developed AltaVista Search, for his technical expertise, sense of humor, and feedback. Megg Bonar and Scott Rogers from Osborne/McGraw Hill for staying sane and getting the details right. Claire Splan from Osborne/McGraw-Hill for her work in pulling all the words together. Sharon Henderson for all her efforts in pulling this book together and working behind the scenes to make sure that the "business" details went through smoothly. And Joella Paquette for her early leadership in getting this book off the ground.

To all the folks in Digital's Corporate Strategy and Technology Group and research labs, especially Bill Strecker and Wendy Caswell, without whose support and initiative this book would not have been started. Also from Digital's Corporate Strategy and Technology Group: Sam Fuller, Bob Supnik, Jay Zager, Jon Braley, and Donna Berard. From Digital's Labs: Brian Reid, Chuck Thacker, Jeremy Dion, Stephen Stuart, Glenn Trewitt, Dick Sites, Paul Flaherty, Mark Manasse, Steve Glassman, Jay Kistler, Robin Landers, Puneet Kumar, Kathy Richardson, Sharon Perl, Annie Warren, Jason Wold, Betsy Sutter, Sanjay Ghemawat, Lance Berc, Andrei Broder, Cynthia Hibbard, Joel Bartlett, Marco Annaratone, Virgil Champlain, David Jefferson, Jean Marie Diaz, Luis Paez, Ty Tressitte, Steve Schneider, Mark Curtis, and others who, while very important, prefer to remain anonymous. Also to the folks in AltaVista Software, Inc. who helped make this book possible, including Ann Killilea, Freddy Mini, Barry Rubinson, and Phil Steffora. And thanks to Harvard MBA students Jeff Watson, Judy Stahl, and Marci Smith.

And especially, thanks to the thousands of people who provided examples of AltaVista use. We wish we could have used all of them.

The Authors

The original AltaVista Search Public Service team from December 1995: *from left to right, front row:* Paul Flaherty, Joella Paquette; *second row:* Annie Warren, David Jefferson; *third row:* Andrei Broder; *back row:* Glenn Trewitt, Louis Monier, Stephen Stuart.

The AltaVista Search Public Service team today: *from left to right, front row:* Eric Asden, Ty Tressitte, Barry Rubinson, Luis Paez, Mark Curtis; *second row:* Jean Marie Diaz, Steve Schneider, Robert Lee; *third row:* Eric Kidd, Jim Lieb; *back row:* Kelly Felkins, Phil Steffora, Louis Monier.

Welcome to *The AltaVista Search Revolution!* Just as the World Wide Web revolutionized the Internet by making a wealth of information easily available to anyone with Web browser software, Digital Equipment Corporation's AltaVista Search Service is revolutionizing the Web by making the information easily available *and* easy to get to directly.

For example, suppose you have a few items left in your refrigerator and want recipes for interesting dishes you could make with them. With a cookbook, you would first have to guess the types or the names of the dishes, then try to find recipes. With AltaVista Search, you simply enter the items that you have on hand and perhaps the word "recipe" as well.

Or, perhaps you are plagued by a few words of what may be a song or a poem or a passage in a book. If you knew the author and knew that it was a "classic" and knew the first words of what's considered a famous quote, you'd use Bartlett's or another reference work. But, often, you don't know who wrote it or when, and these are random words from the middle of something. With AltaVista Search, you just enter the words that you know.

Maybe your computer just crashed and a cryptic error message appeared on the screen as it died. You don't know if it's a hardware or a software problem nor can you even guess what the problem could be. You don't know what documentation to use and where to look in it. You can just enter the error message and let AltaVista Search do the searching for you.

Being able to search everything on the Internet and really find the information you need, when you need it, now *that's revolutionary*. The consequences are enormous not just for you as a searcher for information, but also for anyone who wants their information to be found, and for anyone who is thinking of doing business on the Internet.

The purpose of this book is to help you learn how to take full advantage of AltaVista Search and also how to operate in the new and changing Internet environment, as both an information consumer and an information provider. You can use AltaVista Search as a tool to find long-lost friends and relatives and meet new friends; to check on what your competitors are doing, what your customers are saying, and to find new markets; to complete tonight's homework assignment or do basic research for your doctoral dissertation.

While many search services existed on the Web before AltaVista Search, and more continue to appear, none can match the power, scope, flexibility, and sheer usefulness of AltaVista Search. AltaVista Search will seek out and present to you information that otherwise could have gone unnoticed on computers throughout the world.

The AltaVista Search Revolution will give you a guided tour of AltaVista Search from its origins in Digital Equipment Corporation's Palo Alto, California, laboratories to its current place as the preeminent Internet search service with over 10 million searches each and every day. You'll learn how to effectively use AltaVista Search through explanation and examples of building your own searches. The AltaVista Search A to Z Reference presents dozens of examples of actual AltaVista searches and the interesting information you can uncover using AltaVista Search. Through these examples you'll see that the real significance of AltaVista Search—beyond Digital Equipment Corporation's technical achievements—is how the technology touches people's lives and makes them better informed and more productive.

WHO SHOULD USE THIS BOOK

You should read this book if you want to use the Internet to find anything you want, anytime you want. If you can't find the information you need using AltaVista Search, you won't find it out there. Other search and directory services provide good and useful links to information on the Web or Usenet newsgroups, but AltaVista Search is the one that indexes more of the Web and Usenet than any other search service and indexes *every* word it finds out there. AltaVista Search also contains the largest and most comprehensive index of current newsgroups. With over 30 million total pages of information on the Web and approximately 4.5 million articles posted to Usenet each day, no other search service can come close.

WHAT'S IN THIS BOOK

This book contains the following types of information:

- An introduction to AltaVista Search and Internet Searches.

- Step-by-step instructions and useful descriptions of AltaVista Search features.

- Tips for Webmasters and information providers on how they can take advantage of the power of AltaVista Search.

- The AltaVista Search A to Z Reference, complete with examples and anecdotes.

■ The AltaVista Story, including the inside information about AltaVista Search's development.

Chapter One introduces AltaVista Search itself. We'll describe how Internet search engines and directories work and explain their role in the development of the Internet. Additionally, we'll present the key characteristics that make Alta Vista Search the premier search engine on the Internet.

Chapter Two describes the basics of how to use AltaVista Simple Search. We start with an introduction to the AltaVista home page and briefly explain the important elements. We also discuss how to construct Simple Searches and how to set up searches to get the best results.

Chapter Three introduces AltaVista Advanced Search, which offers more power and options than Simple Search, allowing you to precisely control your searches and narrow your results. We'll show how to use operators and grouping techniques to comb the Internet for nuggets of information. A big part of this chapter will present, through example, how to narrow searches and make them more effective.

Chapter Four presents both Simple and Advanced Searches of Usenet newsgroups. In addition to explaining how newsgroups differ from the World Wide Web, we present techniques to search the 16,000+ newsgroups with their millions of messages.

Chapter Five presents information providers with the tips and techniques necessary to ensure that AltaVista Search indexes their pages effectively. Additionally, we provide pointers with which Webmasters can help their readers find and use their Web pages.

Chapter Six is the AltaVista Search A to Z Reference. We present dozens of subject categories, a brief description of the category, followed by a list of specific search ideas and samples. Stories from AltaVista Search users interspersed throughout the chapter will help you broaden your concept of how you can use AltaVista Search.

Chapter Seven presents the story of how AltaVista Search came to be—how it was possible to create a single tool that can do it all, and how a large company was able to turn an R&D project into such a powerful and useful tool for Internet users everywhere.

WHAT YOU'LL NEED TO USE ALTAVISTA SEARCH

Before you can use AltaVista Search, you'll need to have a computer with an Internet connection and some kind of Web browser software. That's it!

ICONS USED IN THIS BOOK

Throughout this book, you'll see a few icons that indicate special information.

 ip: *You'll see this icon in places that we provide some extra information that will make using AltaVista Search a little easier. Most of this information we've found out through trial and error and want to pass it on to you.*

 ote: *Where you see this icon, you'll find background or supplementary information. This information is not absolutely essential for you to use AltaVista Search, but it will help you better understand AltaVista Search as a whole.*

 emember: *Information following this icon will help remind you of concepts or steps you learned in previous sections or chapters. We provide these little reminders so that you won't have to keep flipping back to other chapters for information.*

Enjoy *The AltaVista Search Revolution!*

1

Introduction to AltaVista Search

Searching the Internet will never be the same! The AltaVista Search revolution has transformed the Internet into a medium that you can use to find the information you want when you want it. You'll never have to slog through unnecessary or irrelevant information to find just the right item you're looking for. Gone are the days of arcane Unix-based commands, the repeated trips to different directories and search engines, and the frustration of knowing that the data you need is probably out there, somewhere—if you could only *find* it. Using a single command in AltaVista, you can search through the World Wide Web or through over 16,000 Usenet newsgroups to find that piece of information you need.

What makes Digital Equipment Corporation's AltaVista Search so special? Scope, speed, and ease of use. AltaVista Search indexes the World Wide Web and Usenet newsgroups and makes that index easily available to the entire Internet community. It provides a single entry point and simple interface—just type a few words and press ENTER to search—to the World Wide Web and 16,000-plus Usenet newsgroups, and gives you quick access to all the information they contain. AltaVista Search empowers you by giving you in seconds information that might otherwise be impossible to find.

Since AltaVista Search debuted, instead of wading through pages and pages of information from hundreds or thousands of sources, you now only have to search one location to quickly find the information you need. AltaVista Search *is* the standard to which all other Internet search tools are compared. If you can't find it using AltaVista Search, it's probably not out there.

This chapter explains why AltaVista Search is so exciting and provides some background to make it easier to see the full significance of the AltaVista Search revolution. First, you will learn how AltaVista differs from other search tools and how it continues to transform the Internet and business in general. Next, you will see how the Internet developed, the immense problems with Internet searches, and other Internet search solutions. Finally, you will learn how AltaVista really does stand alone as *the* Internet search tool.

This knowledge will prepare you for the rest of this book, which describes some of the tools and techniques used to find order in chaos, and you'll see how you can use AltaVista Search to both access and provide access to the information throughout the Internet.

ALTAVISTA SEARCH: THE REVOLUTION!

It's quick . . . it's easy . . . it's convenient . . . it's *here*.

AltaVista Search solves the problems of finding information on the Internet and brings the information right to your desktop. AltaVista Search is *not* just another search service; rather, its scope, speed, and ease of use make it *the* search engine of the Internet.

AltaVista Search's Scope

AltaVista Search, developed in 1995 by Digital Equipment Corporation in its Palo Alto labs, did the unthinkable—it indexed the Internet in a project of unmatched scope. AltaVista Search is the place on the Internet in which documents from across the Internet are cataloged—word by word. Want to find all occurrences of "for whom the bell tolls" on the Internet? AltaVista Search is the place. Want to know which newsgroup postings in the last three days have mentioned your company by name? AltaVista Search will show you.

With the help of Scooter, a program that roams around the Web to collect addresses and information, AltaVista Search doesn't merely index key terms or ideas, but rather collects Web pages, and the pages they connect to, and the pages those pages connect to, and so on across the Internet. As Scooter collects the pages, they're submitted to the indexing software and made available through AltaVista. Anything that Scooter has found, you can find, too, just by typing a word or two into AltaVista Search. Additionally, you can find new information just about as quickly as it's available on the Web, without having to wait for someone to determine where that new information should fit in a database or catalog.

AltaVista Search's Speed

Even beyond the technical achievement of indexing the whole Web, AltaVista Search allows you to search the whole Web remarkably quickly—quicker, in fact, than you can probably find something on your desk. (Well, a *lot* quicker than finding something on our desks.)

With the help of sophisticated software, robust Internet connections, and state-of-the-art Digital Equipment Corporation Alpha workstations, you can search through the entire Internet in less time than it takes to find a file on a personal computer. If you type in a search term, grab your mouse, and click the Submit button, you're likely to have results on your screen before your hand returns to the keyboard. Now that's fast!

AltaVista Search's Ease of Use

All of AltaVista Search's scope and speed would mean nothing if it weren't easy to use. With AltaVista Search, you can use a Simple Search, type in words that interest you, and review the results. It's really that easy. And even with that ease, you still take advantage of the full power and scope of AltaVista. (Simple Search is the one the AltaVista Search developers generally use.) Advanced or power users, or anyone who needs to construct particularly detailed or complex searches, can use AltaVista Search's Advanced Search mode to develop precise search strategies that isolate carefully chosen pieces of information.

SO, WHAT'S SO REVOLUTIONARY, ANYWAY?

AltaVista Search solves the wide range of problems associated with finding information in a resource with the complexity and broad scope of the Internet. With the advent of AltaVista Search, the difficulties involved with cataloging information, developing databases that selectively include words and phrases, as well as the overriding problems with too much available information, are no more. AltaVista Search allows you to selectively and easily get only the information you need, when you need it.

Pretty cool—but what's so revolutionary about a high-powered index? What does AltaVista do that makes it so special? To give you an idea, step back a few paces and look at how the Internet began, how it grew, and how it created a seemingly unwieldy mass of information (unwieldy, of course, until AltaVista came along).

In the Beginning . . .

The Internet, started in 1969 as a Department of Defense research project, connects millions of computers worldwide in a complex and ever-changing network. The synergy of the millions of Internet users provided an incredible store of knowledge and a remarkable capacity for collecting and disseminating information.

Unfortunately, the same diversity that gave the Internet its power also made the organization of the Internet remarkably chaotic. The Internet's almost apocalyptic chaos stemmed from unfettered growth combined with little structure or organization. As prices of computer hardware and network infrastructure fell, more people and more companies jumped on the bandwagon, purchased Internet access, and sought out information. The decentralized design of the Internet meant that this process of adding more computers and smaller networks to the Internet was relatively easy. However, the loosely-woven network design also made it almost impossible to track the growth. For example, computers and whole subnetworks could be added or removed with no notice or warning—and often with few people the wiser.

Additionally, information providers flocked to the Internet as it grew. Just as the growth of the Internet was exponential, so too was the rise in these information sources. Many sites, while useful to those who knew about them, often went unnoticed by others on the Internet due to poor communications, perceived low interest, or other human or technical difficulties. Unfortunately, "if you build it, they will come" didn't always apply. The result was a ton of information that was virtually unusable.

Then Came Information Search Problems . . .

As the Internet grew by leaps and bounds, searching for information went from difficult to virtually impossible. For many people, the Internet was an information nightmare because the available primitive search tools were inadequate for the sheer volume of what the Internet provided. "Information overload" didn't begin to describe the information searching problem that this enormous growth caused on the Web and on Usenet newsgroups.

World Wide Web

As the Internet—or, more specifically, the World Wide Web—grew, many new pages appeared on servers around the world, but there was no mechanism in place to ensure that someone knew about them. Additionally, when older pages were removed from the network or moved to different places, nobody took care of notifying everyone—or even *someone*—of the changes. Seasoned Internet veterans grew accustomed to information sources disappearing, then reappearing elsewhere, but neither veterans nor novices could consistently seek out vanished information sources or reliable replacements without a growing sense of frustration and helplessness.

Even keeping track of new additions to the Internet overwhelmed most users. To this day, many people dedicate substantial amounts of time to keeping track of all the known Internet resources within a particular—increasingly narrowly defined—subject domain. This gloomy picture of the melange of information on the

World Wide Web was quite discouraging for information seekers, but remained far better than the situation for the Usenet discussion groups.

Usenet Newsgroups

Usenet (or network news) discussion groups posed a different set of difficulties for information seekers, including the problems of scope, quantity, and instability. Usenet news grew to its current count of over 16,000 newsgroups, covering literally every topic imaginable. These groups generated millions of messages each day, far beyond the scope of anyone's ability to keep up. Most people couldn't even keep track of the top three or four groups that interested them, let alone the twenty or more that contained information they needed.

As quickly as these Usenet messages appeared, they "expired" and disappeared from the Internet. Usenet messages usually remained accessible for between two and six weeks, at which point they were (and still are) routinely and automatically deleted. Even if someone were to keep up with the new messages as they appeared, the older ones would be disappearing as quickly.

Finding useful information in Usenet or on the Web required perseverance, patience, quick reactions, and the willingness to plow through irrelevant or useless data. Early attempts to solve the enormous information problem helped some, but still didn't offer much relief.

Then Came a Few Solutions . . . (Sort of)

As a result of the growth in Internet users, service providers, available information, and retrieval problems, software engineers and information specialists alike attempted to catalog, index, or otherwise provide improved access to useful sites on the Internet, but with generally limited success. In earlier days, arcane tools—remember Archie, Veronica, and Jughead?—provided information about specific sites on the Internet. Although they were by no means comprehensive, they did offer a starting point to track down data. Skilled Internet users learned to use the existing Internet resources to identify the information they needed.

Out of this mess grew the first attempts to bring order out of chaos. The development moved in two different directions—toward *directories* and *search engines*.

Directories

Internet directories provide hierarchically organized lists of links and lend themselves to browsing. Directories, such as Yahoo!, present a carefully categorized, apparently logically-structured facade to World Wide Web-based information. Laborious manual categorization and indexing provide information seekers easy access to select sites.

Of course, sites that haven't been cataloged can't be found, and with the rate of World Wide Web growth, there isn't a team that can keep up with cataloging new sites as quickly as they appear. Additionally, manual catalogs are fairly limited in cross-references—it just is not possible to anticipate all of the potentially related topics and to provide pointers to other areas of a catalog to cover all contingencies.

Search Engines

Search engines maintain a database with links to Internet resources and are great for quickly identifying a specific resource. For example, if you are searching for information about movies, you can swiftly search for any sites that discuss movies without having to wait for an individual to catalog the site.

Search engines collect information about World Wide Web sites and allow seekers to search for specific data. The downside is that a searchable database of the whole Internet is enormous and requires significant computing power to be able to build an index and present that information to the Internet community.

As a result, most search engines index only *some* of the words or *some* of the information from *some* of the sites. Indexing more than just the key words describing a site often poses an overwhelming technological burden for the service providers. Searchers could find anything that's in the database, but, of course, could not find anything that wasn't there.

These early indexing attempts were less than ideal because of the impossibility of anticipating all user needs. While it was possible to index the "key" words of documents, in addition to titles and descriptions, guessing exactly what words would be useful to searchers wasn't possible . . . or was it?

Then Came AltaVista . . .

AltaVista Search applies advanced software technologies, high-bandwidth networking, and the raw computing power of 64-bit Alpha workstations to the immensity of the Internet—it's the classic irresistible-force-meets-immovable-object situation. The Alpha's irresistible force won out, and impressively!

AltaVista Search has become the standard for the Internet—the standard against which all other search engines are measured. The success of AltaVista since its debut in December 1995 was so incredible, even by Internet standards of instant popularity, that Digital has recently launched an entire business based on the technology:

AltaVista OnSite Computing. AltaVista OnSite Computing, just like its namesake on the Internet, is designed to make the Internet and computing in general easier and more productive for everyone.

Now, in addition to continuing to provide the original comprehensive service at no charge to the Internet community, AltaVista Search also powers the Web searches of everyone's favorite directory services, including Yahoo! AltaVista Search is also making inroads to the realm of the personal computer—in summer of 1996 tens of thousands of people downloaded the first early technology sampler of AltaVista Search for Windows 95 computers. Why this level of excitement? Simply put, because of the revolutionary effectiveness of AltaVista Search.

Welcome to the Revolution!

Before the AltaVista researchers developed AltaVista Search, you had to keep track of Web addresses, record facts and names, and keep up with Internet developments just to find the information you sought. When you use AltaVista Search, you need only enter a few words and let AltaVista Search do the remembering for you. It's remarkably powerful, completely easy to use, and the most effective and powerful information retrieval tool you've ever found. The next few chapters will show you how to use this tool to its full potential, as well as how to use AltaVista Search more effectively and in ways you hadn't imagined. Follow along at **http://altavista.digital.com/** and join the AltaVista Search revolution!

2

Getting Started
with AltaVista
Search

Using AltaVista Search to find anything on the Web or in newsgroups—anywhere in the world—is as easy as typing a name or term. While you may be familiar with other Internet search services, you'll find that AltaVista Search is very different. AltaVista Search provides particularly useful results—using either the Simple Search, covered in this chapter, or the Advanced Search, addressed in Chapter 3—that you cannot get with other tools on the Internet.

This chapter is divided into three main parts. The first part, "About the AltaVista Search Home Page," takes you to AltaVista Search and introduces its features. This section also thoroughly describes the options you have in Simple Search and how to try them out. It is *simple*, so the choices are narrowed, but this tour should be helpful.

The second part, "Doing Simple Searches," takes you through the process of simple searches. In this section you'll find step-by-step instructions on completing a search and choosing how much information to get back from your query. To follow along with the instructions, you'll need to be connected to the Internet and have Web browser software (e.g., Netscape, Internet Explorer, or a comparable tool).

The third part, "Honing Your Simple Search Skills," provides eleven key elements that will help you improve your search skills and therefore your search results. We tried to give you a top ten list, but didn't want to throw anything away.

 ote: *AltaVista Search provides comprehensive results—it finds everything, However, it takes some practice to focus the results so you get just what you're looking for. This chapter will show you how to find anything on the Internet and how to keep from becoming overwhelmed with information—avoiding the old "drinking from a firehose" problem. If you don't think that being flooded with information about a given topic is a bad thing, you just try sorting through 20,000 recipes to find out what to make for dinner.*

ABOUT THE ALTAVISTA SEARCH HOME PAGE

Let's take a look at the AltaVista Search home page. To get to the AltaVista Search home page, you'll need to launch your Web browser and type **http://altavista.digital.com/** in the location window. You can also use the URL

(Uniform Resource Locator) **http://www.altavista.digital.com/** to connect to AltaVista Search. Both connect to precisely the same information, though one requires less typing. In this book, we'll use **http://altavista.digital.com/** because it just seems more logical—you can use whichever one seems more convenient.

The AltaVista Search home page provides you with all the tools you'll need for Simple searches of Web pages and of Usenet newsgroups. (Advanced searches of the Web are covered in Chapter 3, and both Simple and Advanced searches of Usenet newsgroups in Chapter 4.) Figure 2-1 shows you the whole set of AltaVista Search home page features, which are discussed in detail in the rest of this chapter.

■ The *Navigation Bar* across the top of the page contains five options: OnSite Knowledge, Advanced Search, Simple Search, Products, and Help. These are hypertext links that let you jump to different parts of AltaVista Search by clicking on each of the words. *About the Navigation Bar* provides a full overview of using the different words shown in this bar.

■ *Tip* changes fairly frequently and always provides good suggestions about using AltaVista Search. You should try these tips as you notice them because practicing will make it easier for you to search on your own.

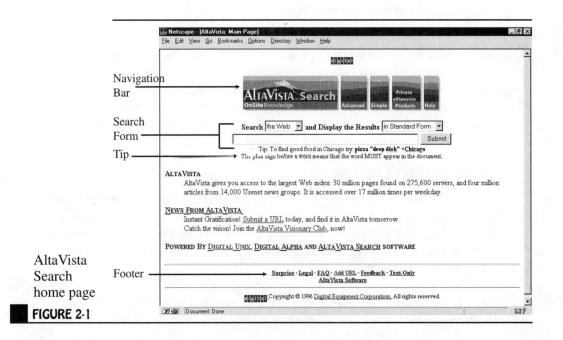

AltaVista
Search
home page

FIGURE 2-1

- *Search Form* lets you choose what to search and how to present the results. It also gives you a place to input your search criteria.

- *Footer* information is fairly straightforward.

  - *Surprise* sends you to a menu of categories. Select a category and get a random link that is guaranteed to be worth the price you paid for it.

  - *Legal* gives you the standard disclaimers. You should probably read them. They are short, clear, and painless.

  - *Tips* is also very useful—you can get the inside scoop from AltaVista Search pros about gleaning the best nuggets from the Internet.

  - *Add URL* lets you submit a specific URL to AltaVista Search (more about this in Chapter 5).

  - *Feedback* lets you tell the AltaVista Search development team what you think.

  - The *Text-Only link* takes you to a page with all of the search capabilities but without the graphics.

  - *AltaVista Software* provides information about other applications of AltaVista Search technology.

 ote: *AltaVista Search's Text-Only page might be very useful if your link to the Internet is pretty slow and you find yourself having to wait for the AltaVista Search Menu to load on your computer. You get all the capabilities, but you don't get to see the graphics—probably a good trade off from a time-management perspective. Certainly if you're using a text-only browser, like Lynx, the Text-Only page is a better starting point than the regular Simple Search page.*

Your Navigation Choices

The Navigation Bar at the top of the AltaVista Search home page, shown in Figure 2-2, is your gateway to AltaVista Search. If you are viewing a page without that logo, you've left AltaVista Search and are somewhere out on the Internet. (Of course, if you are, it means that your search worked and you're on track to getting the information you were looking for, right?)

 ote: *If you choose text-only mode, you will not see the graphical Navigation Bar, but you will still see links to each of the different parts of AltaVista Search.*

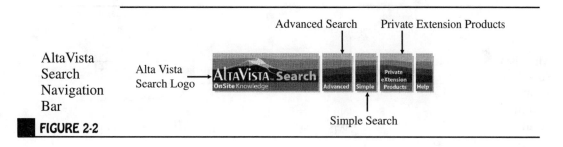

AltaVista Search Navigation Bar

FIGURE 2-2

To navigate around AltaVista Search, just click on:

- *AltaVista Search Logo* (at the left) to go to a page with general information about AltaVista Search.

- *Advanced Search* to go to the Advanced Search page. You'll read about this in Chapter 3.

- *Simple Search* to take you back to the home page or, for all practical purposes, to the Simple Search location.

- *Private Extension Products* gives you the chance to take a piece of AltaVista Search home with you. If you've been losing sleep since you started this book wondering how to use this cool technology in other ways, you can relax now. Digital's way ahead of you. You'll find software to download and all kinds of information about how AltaVista Search technology is being applied to other information retrieval problems.

- *Help* to get—you guessed it—help. There's good information here for those willing to read the instructions. Of course, if you're reading this book, you're already getting help.

About the Simple Search Form

The Search Form is the key to using AltaVista Search; it is the feature you'll use to make your search requests. When you first bring up the AltaVista Search home page, you'll see a search form that looks like Figure 2-3.

- *Search Selector* allows you to choose whether you want to search the Web or Usenet newsgroups.

- *Output Selector* allows you to choose the amount of detail you get in your search results. You'll see three choices: Standard, Compact, and Detailed.

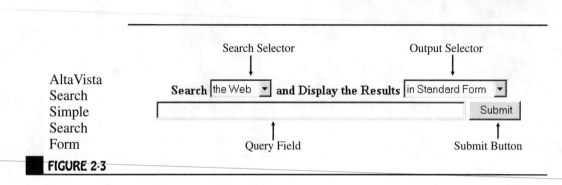

AltaVista Search Simple Search Form

FIGURE 2-3

For Web searches, selecting Standard or Detailed from the drop-down box yields the same result: detailed information about the pages. Selecting Compact, as the name indicates, provides less detailed search results.

ote: *"Standard" in this context refers to the default setting. The Standard (or default) setting when searching the Web is Detailed. The Standard (default) setting when searching Usenet (Chapter 4) is Compact.*

■ *Query field* is where you type in the search criteria, including significant words and any other pertinent information. Your search criteria will be visible and editable in this field even after you submit your query, so you'll easily be able to edit and revise your query, and yes, you'll want to. As you'll see later in this chapter, even a minor tweak can make a world of difference.

■ *Submit Button* is what you click on to submit the query for search. (On some browsers, you can also hit ENTER.)

Standard Form

Standard Form always gives you the default format in AltaVista Search and is generally a very good choice. When you submit a Web query with Standard Form selected, you get back a list of the top ten matches and some additional information about each of them. The list of results provides plenty of information about the links so you can tell what's interesting and relevant. It includes the following items, as shown in Figure 2-4.

■ *Word count* tells approximately how many times each of your search terms was found in the AltaVista Search index—that is, in the Internet.

- *Ignored* lists which of your search terms were too common to be useful and are therefore not represented in the results.

- *Approximate number of matches* indicates roughly how many documents AltaVista Search found that match your criteria.

- *Title* of each item is a direct link to the document. This *title* might not appear in the body of the document but is the name that the author has given to the document.

- *First text from the document* (or other text that the author specifically designated) gives you a brief idea of what information is in the document. See Chapter 5 for more information about specifying abstracts or descriptions.

- *URL* (or Web address) appears in the form of a link. With practice, you can use the URL to access useful information about the site and the possible content, such as the information source and the actual name of the document. Reading information into URLs isn't always reliable but often provides some useful data. For example, a URL with *.com* in it is probably from some sort of commercial site, just as a URL with *.edu* indicates an educational institution. A URL with *digital.com* in it would

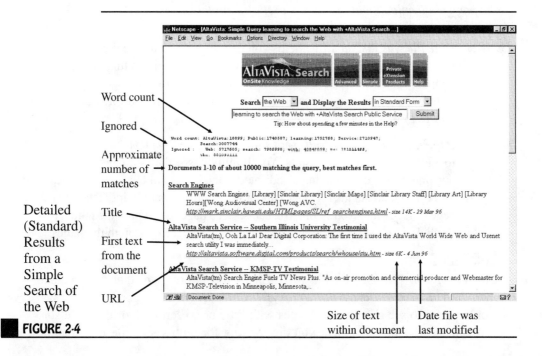

Detailed
(Standard)
Results
from a
Simple
Search of
the Web

FIGURE 2-4

probably be a better source of information about Alpha computers than a URL with */personal/opinions/computers/Alpha.*

 ote: *Sometimes you'll see several URLs associated with a single abstract or description. Although they share identical abstracts, the content of each of the URLs is different in some way, so each might offer useful information. The only way to tell how significant the differences are is to select each of the links and compare them.*

- *Size of the text within document* shows how much disk space the actual text of the document requires. Remember that a Web *page* is not a page in the ordinary sense of the word but is a distinct document or file that can be any size—from just a few characters to an entire book.

 ote: *Web pages can consist entirely of text, or they can include sound or graphics or video, in any mix and in a wide variety of formats. Graphics or other multimedia elements significantly increase the size of the page, but AltaVista Search only indexes the text portions of Web pages. Graphics or multimedia elements included from the document significantly increase the length of time it takes the page to download, but they are not reflected in this number.*

- *Date file was last modified* helps you determine how useful the information might be. For example, if you want details on this month's happenings in the Middle East, you won't want to go to a page that was last updated a year ago because it won't have the current information you're looking for.

- *Page numbers of the results* (not shown in Figure 2-4) lets you move to additional screens of results. You'll initially see the first page of ten documents. Page numbering is indicated at the bottom of the screen by the letter *p* (which stands for **p**age) and a series of numbers to indicate what page of the results you're on. You can select a page by clicking the number or clicking Next (or Previous) to move back and forth through the pages.

Compact Form

Compact Form provides only a fragment of the information that the Detailed (Standard for Web searches) Form provides. Compact Form is a good choice if you would prefer to see all of your choices with little or no scrolling or if you're sure you can identify the document you are looking for with very little information.

(Heavy users of Compact Form tend to be pretty good at *Name That Tune* as well.) The information Compact Form provides is very similar to that of Standard—some of the data is truncated or omitted, but you get all the basics, and, of course, the links take you to the very same document on the Internet.

Making AltaVista Search Your Home Page

If you find that you use AltaVista Search frequently and are getting tired of typing **http://altavista.digital.com/** every time, you could make the AltaVista Search Service your home page. Changing your home page is slightly different, but equally easy, in almost any browser. If you use Netscape Navigator, do the following:

1. Open Netscape.

2. Go to Options | General Preferences.

3. Select the Appearance Tab.

4. Under On Startup Launch, select Netscape Browser.

5. Under Start With, select Home Page Location.

6. Enter **http://altavista.digital.com** in the field under Home Page Location. Your dialog box should look like this:

7. Click OK.

8. To save this configuration change, select Options | Save Options.

Now, whenever you launch Netscape you will start with the AltaVista Search home page. You can also just click the home icon from the toolbar to return to AltaVista Search at any time.

If you use Microsoft's Internet Explorer, do the following:

1. Open Internet Explorer.

2. Enter **http://altavista.digital.com** in the Address field at the top of your window.

3. Go to View | Options, and select the Start and Search Pages tab.

4. Select Start Page in the drop-down box.

5. Click Use Current to make AltaVista Search your new home page.

6. If you want to set your Internet Search page to be AltaVista Search as well, select Search Page in the drop-down box and click Use Current again.

DOING SIMPLE SEARCHES

This section walks you through your first search with AltaVista Search. Actually, it might not be your first one, but we'll try to make it the more successful one. To start using AltaVista Search, you should have an Internet connection and browser software. It's also going to help if you don't have an appointment in the next couple of hours because AltaVista Search makes it even easier than before to immerse yourself in the Internet and lose all track of time.

1. Connect to the Internet. This means to dial into your Internet Service Provider (ISP) if you have to (or just get a cup of coffee and rejoice in being able to use your company's Internet connection so freely!).

2. Open your browser.

3. Connect to AltaVista Search by typing **http://altavista.digital.com** in the Location field, which is near the top of your browser window.

4. Press ENTER.

You're here! Welcome to AltaVista Search! (If you don't see something very similar to Figure 2-1, check to make sure that you typed the address correctly.)

Simple Search with Standard Output

The most basic search is a Simple Search with standard output. To try one of these, do the following:

1. Leave the selections of Search the Web and Standard Form as they stand.

2. Click in the Query field (that long skinny area just begging to be filled with your search terms).

3. Type the word or words you want to search for. Try using **tornado**.

4. Click Submit or press ENTER.

Some results from this search are shown in Figure 2-5.

There you go—Internet sites with *tornado*, complete with brief information about the titles, descriptions, and dates. AltaVista Search even tried to guess what you really wanted to see first, based on where the word appears in the documents, and presented those documents at the top of the list. To learn how to tweak your search to give much more targeted and useful information about tornadoes or other things, check out "Honing Your Simple Search Skills" later in this chapter.

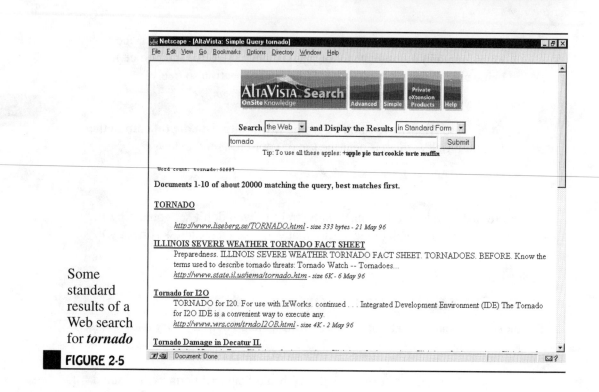

Some
standard
results of a
Web search
for *tornado*

FIGURE 2-5

Saving Results

If you've just conducted a great search and want to save your results, you
have two options. First, you could save the actual list of links (in the groups
of ten that AltaVista Search presents). This choice would be good for putting
together a customized list of HTML documents that you find useful. You'd
be able to incorporate any or all of the pages generated by AltaVista Search
into your document.

Second, you could just bookmark the search. If you do that, your
browser saves the search settings and information, but not the actual links.
Each time you return to your bookmark, the browser resubmits the search
to AltaVista Search and you get the latest and greatest list of links. (We'd
recommend this choice, since you asked.)

Saving a Search

To save the results of your search in Netscape or Internet Explorer (and in most other browsers as well), do the following:

1. Conduct the search in AltaVista Search.

2. Go to File | Save As.

3. Select a filename and location for your document and click OK.

Bookmarking a Search

If you use Internet Explorer, do the following:

1. Conduct the search in AltaVista Search.

2. Go to Favorites | Add Favorite.

Your favorite has now been saved under your Favorites menu and you can go back to it at any time.

If you use Netscape, do the following:

1. Conduct the search in AltaVista Search.

2. Go to Bookmarks | Add Bookmark.

Your bookmark has now been saved under your Bookmarks menu, and you can go back to it at any time.

Refer to your browser's help menu for more information about bookmarking and managing your list of favorites. Of course, you could always just use AltaVista Search to find the help. Try searching for **managing bookmarks netscape** or **managing favorites explorer**.

HONING YOUR SIMPLE SEARCH SKILLS

This section provides you with some basic techniques to use the AltaVista search service effectively.

 ote: *Please pardon this interruption: We'll be the first to admit that you can get pretty good results just shooting in the dark. A little time spent reading the manual, however, improved our success rate tremendously.*

You're welcome to find what you want using a hit-or-miss approach—just typing words in the Search Form and seeing what results come up. That's what most people do today. But if you understand how AltaVista Search works, you can focus your search very precisely and use—and reuse—the results in creative and valuable ways. Doing so allows you to take advantage of the full resources of the Internet to meet your needs—business or personal.

 ote: *AltaVista Search searches number millions a day and the total continues to grow at a remarkable rate.*

Before you dive into the techniques for improving your search results, you'll need to consider exactly *what* you consider a successful search. Is it one that returns a very limited number of results so you can look through all of them? Or one that retrieves the most appropriate matches and places them at the top of a (potentially very long) list?

If you're coming to AltaVista Search with experience in more traditional library searches or even with experience with other Internet search engines, you'll probably start in the short-list camp. We suggest that you try to move into the top-of-the-list group. There's no point in working as hard as you need to work for a short list when AltaVista Search can usually take care of presenting the best matches at the top of the list (and who really cares about the last several thousand matches anyway?).

 ote: *Keep in mind that the AltaVista Search developers are continually improving and refining the system—adding features and making adjustments to provide optimum performance for everyone. Some of the specifics provided here—such as the number of matches returned when you do a search—may change* *over time, but the underlying principles, embedded in the software, will remain constant.*

While there are plenty of additional techniques and tricks that will make searches with AltaVista Search easier, these will give you a good start. Because AltaVista Search is quite different from a library card catalog or most other Internet search engines, you'll probably need a little practice to get the most out of it. We did.

The following sections discuss specific techniques to help you use AltaVista Search more effectively:

- Using rare words

- Using all words that might matter

- Using phrases when you know the exact word order

- Using punctuation and spaces

- Using capitalization

- Using accent marks where applicable

- Using wildcards when you aren't sure of the exact word

- Searching according to structural elements

- Requiring specific words or phrases

- Excluding specific words or phrases

- Combining elements in your searches

Using Rare Words

Using rare words is a great way to improve your search results. If what you want to find can be identified by an unusual name or term, you will be able to quickly isolate your target. If you can use an unusual term or proper name, you will have fewer matches to sift through before you find the information you need. (If you choose to use well-done words instead of rare, we're not responsible for the condition of your results. They may be dried out and tough.)

Using rare words in your search is important because of the way the search service works. When you search for a specific word, AltaVista Search checks through an index that contains every word found on over 30 million Web pages that reside on over 275,000 servers around the world. If the word you asked for is common, it probably has appeared many times. For instance, if you search for the word **music**, you'll find over one million documents. You've now gained a piece of trivia, but aren't likely to be able to scan through all one million documents to isolate the ones with the information you want. However, searching for **musicals** gives you about 3,000 documents—a much more manageable number but still a little hard to peruse. Getting as specific as possible and entering the rare word **Evita** gives you more precisely focused selections of which several of the top ten are obviously relevant.

The more precise you can be about what you are looking for by using rare terms, the better your results will be. Some samples of using rare words rather than common ones include *collie* instead of *dog* or *pet, Dilbert* instead of *comic strip,* or *hyperactivity* rather than *behavior.* Keep in mind that, in this context, how common or rare a word is does not depend on general usage but rather on what actually appears on the World Wide Web. For example, the words *computer* and *Internet* appear much more frequently on the Web than they do in your library card catalog.

Using All Words That Might Matter

Entering all words that might matter is another way of improving search results. Sometimes you can search for information using a single rare term; however, in many instances, you'll need to enter a *series* of words to get the results you're looking for.

The question, then, is how to determine what words to include in the search query. You can do this in two ways: entering a series of rare or uncommon words that pertain to your query, or entering your query as a question.

Entering a Series of Rare Words

You can enter any series of words in any sequence when you're doing a Simple Search. The quickest way to do a search is to enter a series of rare words in the Query field. For example, if you want information about the capital of Alaska, simply enter **capital Alaska** or **Alaska capital.** The AltaVista Search search engine looks for all the Web pages that refer to *capital* and *Alaska.* Web pages that contain both terms appear near the top of the list, while pages that refer to only one or the other are ranked lower in the list.

 Note: *The best way, of course, is to find out what the capital is and then enter Juneau.*

Entering Your Query as a Question

You don't have to use any particular format to enter your query—just type in the whole question you want answered. How can ordinary questions yield useful results? AltaVista Search focuses on the relatively rare words in the query and discards the common words. For example, you can enter a query as **What is the capital of Alaska?** AltaVista Search searches for information using the less common words in the question—in this case, *capital* and *Alaska*—and ignores common words such as *what*, *is*, *the*, and *of* for the purposes of selecting the most likely matches. You'll see what words were used and ignored immediately above the results. Then AltaVista Search ranks the rarest words at the top of your list of results and presents the results to you.

 ote: *AltaVista Search doesn't really know it's a question at all—your query is just a bunch of words to AltaVista Search. However, phrasing the query as a question is useful if you aren't sure how you want to narrow the results or if you're having problems finding good words to use.*

Using Phrases When You Know the Exact Word Order

Another way to improve your search efforts is to use quotation marks to indicate a specific phrase. A phrase is any set of words that appear in a specific order. For example, if you entered the words **to be or not to be**, you would get no results at all because the words are all so common. Each of those words appears tens of millions of times—too frequently to be of any use. However, if you entered those same words using quotation marks, you would get about forty matches—all of them Web pages that include that complete phrase. You could narrow the search even further by including more words within the quotation marks, such as **"to be or not to be, that is the question"**, which will lead you straight to Web pages about Shakespeare's works along with pages that used the quotation, probably out of context, for some reason.

While other search engines discard common English words like *a* and *the* and phrases like *to be or not to be* to conserve space, AltaVista Search saves every one of them. That's what makes it possible to do exact searches for complete phrases and sentences. Used in combination with other words and commands, searching for exact phrases is a valuable tool for narrowing searches, not to mention for looking up quotations.

Using Punctuation and Spaces

Another way to improve your search is by using punctuation and spaces carefully. AltaVista Search indexes only words—not spaces or punctuation marks. AltaVista Search considers a word to be any group of letters and digits, while spaces indicate the end of one word and the beginning of the next.

When you type in a query using just words separated by spaces, those words are treated as separate entities, and their order makes no difference. When you include punctuation in your simple query, you also link those words together in that specific order to form phrases. That means that words connected with any punctuation (e.g., comma, period, colon, or semicolon) are treated as phrases—just as they would be if the same string of words was included inside double quotation marks.

AltaVista Search's approach to punctuation has several benefits. For instance, many people are inconsistent in their use of hyphens, slashes, and other such marks in product names and model numbers. When you use AltaVista Search to find such terms, you don't have to try to imagine all the possible variants of punctuation and search for all of them. You can enter one of them, and the results will include all of them, giving them all equal weight. For instance, AltaVista Search would treat *486-DX, 486/DX,* and *"486 DX"* as identical. However, *486DX* is different—it's one word, not two. To find all possible variants, you might search for **486-DX 486DX**.

Using Capitalization

In addition to using punctuation and spaces carefully, you should think about how you can use capitalization. AltaVista Search is case sensitive, but only when you want it to be. When it indexes text, it preserves the fact that certain letters are capital letters and that others are lowercase. The word *RED* is indexed differently and therefore shows up differently from the words *Red* and *red*.

If you enter your query with all lowercase letters, you will get matches for all instances of those words, regardless of capitalization. If you enter **red**, AltaVista Search will return hits for pages with *RED*, *Red*, *rEd*, *reD*, and so on. On the other hand, if you include capitalization in your query, you will only get hits that exactly match that pattern of capitalization. *RED* will only give you matches of *RED* and not *red* or any other variant. This approach has three important benefits. First, you can easily search for trade names where the word may be common but the capitalization is unique, such as *AltaVista*. You can also easily distinguish between proper nouns and ordinary nouns, such as *Turkey* the country and *turkey* the bird, *Frank* the name and *frank* the adjective, and *Who* the rock group and *who* the pronoun. Second, you can easily search for all variations of capitalization of a particular word with a single query entry in lowercase, rather than having to enter all possible permutations. Finally, special capitalization can make the difference between a successful or unsuccessful search. For example, a search for **next** yields nothing because the word is so common. However, a search for **NeXT**, the company, returns ample appropriate matches.

In brief, if you are not sure about the capitalization of a word, use all lowercase letters. And if you are really really positive, include the capital letters to help narrow your search.

Using Accent Marks Where Applicable

Because AltaVista Search preserves all the accents in all languages that use the Latin alphabet, you can include accent marks in your queries to help narrow the search. An accented word used in a query forces an exact match on the entire word, while an unaccented word matches with all accented and unaccented variants, just as a capitalized word forces an exact match of the capitalization while a lowercase word matches all occurrences with those letters in a row—in any combination of capitals and lowercase.

For example, if you use *Éléphant* in a query, you will match only the French spelling for the pachyderm. However, if you do not enter accents in the Query field (and it could be difficult for you to enter them, depending on your browser, keyboard, and computer system), you can always leave off the accents, thereby matching both the French and English spellings.

Making Character Substitutions

Most character substitutions are fairly straightforward, allowing you to type non-English characters. If you're searching for any letter with an accent, umlaut, slash through it, or other diacritical mark, remove the mark. This applies to *a, c, e, i, n, o, u, y,* in upper and lower case. Additionally, *æ* becomes "ae", and the German sharp *s* becomes "ss". The *eth* (a *D* with a slash through it) becomes *d,* and thorn (a *D* on a stick) becomes "th". Table 2-1 shows the substitutions, followed by the original characters for which the substitution is valid.

AltaVista Search
OnSite Knowledge | Advanced | Simple | Private eXtension Products | Help

Original Characters	Substitution
Æ	AE
Á Â À Å Ã Ä	A
Ç	C
Ð	D
É Ê È Ë	E
Í Î Ì Ï	I
Ñ	N
Ó Ô Ò Ø Õ Ö	O
Þ	TH
Ú Û Ù Ü	U
Ý	Y
æ	ae
á â à å ã ä	a
ç	c
é ê è ë	e
ð	d
í î ì ï	I
ñ	n
ó ô ò ø õ ö	o
ß	ss
þ	th
ú û ù ü	u
ý ÿ	y

AltaVista Search special character substitutions

TABLE 2-1

Using Wildcards When You Aren't Sure of the Exact Word

Another way to broaden your search is to use *wildcards,* which are simply placeholders for missing letters. You can replace missing characters or missing words with an asterisk (*) to get hits on any terms that include variants on the base word. For example, if you search for **colo*r**, you'll get matches for both the British spelling *colour* and the American *color.*

You might use wildcards to catch the plural as well as the singular form of a noun, or different tenses of the same verb, or other grammatical variants and compounds.

 ote: *Wildcards may broaden your search too much and give you more information than you really want. If you're using wildcards and have too many results to manage, try omitting the wildcard or adding a rare term.*

Because of the number of people who use AltaVista Search and the computing power it takes to plow through the whole AltaVista Search index to match a general wildcard, asterisks are somewhat limited in AltaVista Search. You can use an asterisk in AltaVista Search only after three characters, or as a placeholder for up to five unknown lowercase characters.

Another possible use of an asterisk is in a phrase, separated from other words by a space or punctuation. This is particularly useful when searching for a quotation when there's a word you are unsure of. For instance, in response to the query "**one if * land**", AltaVista Search will check for phrases in which the first two words are *one if* and the last word is *land* and only one word separates the beginning from the end. Hence it would match *one if by land, one if over land, one if on land,* and so forth. This approach could help you determine the correct quotation, if that's your objective, or it could also help you find instances where the author, intentionally or not, made a mistake of that kind.

N ote: *Sending "gotcha" messages to the authors of Web pages with this kind of mistake is generally considered to be in poor taste.*

While there will be plenty of occasions when you need to use wildcards to fill out parts of words you don't know, by doing so you broaden your search and could get tens of thousands of matches—possibly too many to be useful. A search for **sing*** will give you such variants as *singer, sings,* and *singing.* But it will also give you *single, singled, singe,* and *singular.* So if you need to use a wildcard, make sure that your query includes other elements, such as phrases and rare words, that will help narrow the results to what you really want or that will help bring the results you want to the top of the list.

Searching According to Structural Elements

You can help improve your search results by searching according to structural elements. Web pages and newsgroup documents have unique structural elements—such as titles, headings, and images—that AltaVista Search saves along with the text. Because a particular term might appear in a Web address (URL), in the name of a newsgroup, or in a graphic, you can also search for information in these elements as well as in the document body. Structural elements may also (depending on what they are) appear in the document body.

AltaVista Search lets you search for nine kinds of Web page structural elements, as shown in the following table. These include *text, title, link, anchor, url, host, domain, image,* and *applet* (a mini-program within a Web page). (Others may be added in the future. Check the online help file for updates.) All of these structure-based searches follow the same general format: one word in lowercase, followed by a colon and then by the word or phrase that is of interest to you.

Element	At-a-Glance Description	How to Enter the Search Information
text:	Restricts the search to the body of the document. If you use *text:*, you will be able to see the words that match your query.	text:"Elvis sightings"
title:	Searches only for the part of the document that the creator explicitly labeled as a title. Titles show up in the top bar or title bar of browsers, rather than in the text itself. When you view the results of a query, this is the word or phrase that appears first for each item, as a hypertext link.	title:"Blue Suede Shoes"
link:	Searches only for a hypertext link (the URL) embedded in the document.	link:elvis.com
anchor:	Searches only for the visible part of a hypertext link (the words you click). You could search for **anchor:"Click here"** and get thousands of hits.	anchor:Elvis
url:	Searches for pages that have these words as part of their address (URL).	url:http://elvis.fan.com /graceland/

Element	At-a-Glance Description	How to Enter the Search Information
host:	Searches only on the host name of the system where the pages reside. It is similar to the *url:* element, but it doesn't look at the complete URL—it just checks the computer name.	host:elvis.com
domain:	Searches only on the domain itself—the last part of the host name. It is similar to the *url:* and *host:* elements, but it doesn't look at anything except the last part.	domain:com
image:	Searches for the address (URL) of an image or picture.	image:elvis.gif
applet:	Searches only for the names or addresses of applets, which are small programs embedded in Web pages.	applet:king

text:

The structure element *text:* will search for any regular text in the document. Not links, not addresses—just plain text.

title:

The structure element *title:* refers to the part of a document that the HTML document author labeled as the title. However, these titles may not appear in the text of the document that you see with your browser. When the title is accurate and descriptive, it focuses on what is most important in a Web page and is a very good way to find the information you want.

Title searches will generally be more specific and selective than more general ones. If the pages you are trying to find include certain words or phrases in the text or use standard naming convention for titles, you can find them quickly. For instance, **title:"Fab Four"** would bring up any documents with the phrase *Fab Four* in the title. Keep in mind, though, that this example would not find any documents with "Fab Four" in the body of the document but not in the title.

link:

The structural element *link:* means a hypertext link—a URL or Web address embedded in the text. This address is hidden in the background behind what's known as an *anchor*—the highlighted text that you click on to connect to that hidden address. If you wanted to search for all documents that link to the White House, you could search for **link: http://www.whitehouse.gov**. If you specifically wanted to find pages that link to the White House for Kids page, try searching for **link:http://www.whitehouse.gov/WH/kids/html/kidshome.html**.

Finding pages by link provides two main advantages. First, you can identify how many documents link to a certain page and, second, you can find all links regardless of how the author identified the anchor in the text. Searching for **link:www.altavista.digital.com** would be quite useful for catching all links to AltaVista Search, regardless of how the link is referenced in the text.

anchor:

If you're particularly concerned with the way readers see a link, the structural element *anchor:* returns pages based on the highlighted links you click. If you remember seeing a specific item in a list and want to get back to the page that had such a list, the anchor tag would be a good place to start. You could search for **anchor:AltaVista** to find all pages that have an anchor that points specifically to *AltaVista*, as opposed to those pages that link to a *great search service* or to *"Alta Vista."*

R **emember:**   *If you're looking for a URL, you'll probably use* link:, *whereas if you're looking for the actual text that people would select, you'll use* anchor:.

url:, host:, and domain:

The structural elements *url:, host:,* and *domain:* are very closely related. They each look at the addresses of the pages themselves. The element *url:* looks at the complete address—the domain name as well as any directory or filenames that follow it. The element *host:* looks at the domain name of the system where the pages reside. The element *domain:* looks only at the last part of the name, such as *.com, .edu, .fr.,* or *.au.* Searching for something like **url:modems.html** would find pages that have that filename, perhaps after some directory names. A search for **host:yoursite.com** would show all pages from your site that AltaVista Search has indexed. A search for

domain:de would show all pages from Germany and **domain:fr** would show all pages from France.

Carefully using *host:* and *domain:*, when they apply, is much more efficient than using *url:,* and it can speed up your searches. For example, if you are looking for information on Digital Equipment Corporation Web sites, you could look for **url:digital**. However, that search would also find things like **http://www.casio.com/watches/digital/prices.htm**. It's tempting to search for **url:www.digital.com** to make sure that Casio doesn't show up, but a more efficient way of accomplishing the same result would be to search for **host:digital**. This result still excludes Casio, but without having to look through every complete URL in AltaVista Search. AltaVista Search also indexes the names of graphic or image files.

image:

The structural element *image:* looks for the address or name of an image. If image files were always logically named, a search for **image:pluto** would return the list of Web pages that have pictures of the planet, the Roman god, or the cartoon character. For a number of reasons, many images have quite cryptic names and are unlikely to show up in *image:* searches.

You could use the *image:* element to find examples of image files of a particular type. For instance, **image:gif** matches millions of Web pages that include .GIF images. And **image:star*.jp*** provides a list of images with names that begin with *star* and are in JPEG format.

applet:

The element *applet:** returns a list of all the sites that have *applets*—small programs embedded in an HTML document. An applet has both a URL and a name, so you could search using *link:* if you know the text of the link. However, if you only know the first word of the name, you can search using *applet:*, for example, **applet:game***. If you find a really great applet and are considering using it on your home page, you could search using the format *applet:thefilename* to see what sites are already using it.

If you are interested in finding samples of other kinds of multimedia files, your best approach is to do a structured search for files that include the usual file extension name in the address. In other words, search for **link:qt** or **link:avi** for QuickTime and AVI movie files, respectively.

Requiring Specific Words or Phrases

Another way to improve your search results is to require certain words or phrases. Remember that queries with two or more words produce results that contain any of the words requested. For example, the query **lefthanded politician** would give a count of all documents that have either word in them, which is a much higher number than the number of documents that contain both those words.

You can tell AltaVista Search that a particular word must be present by putting a "+" before the search word, such as the query **+lefthanded politician**. This query would show all pages that have the word *lefthanded,* and pages with the word *politician* as well would appear at the top of the list. The phrase **+lefthanded +politician** would match only pages that included *both* words (but not necessarily in that order, or even near one another).

You might also want to use the plus sign to affect the ranking of documents. For instance, if you search for **albatross boat fishing**, you'll find that documents that have several instances of *albatross* (a relatively rare word) near the beginning could come out higher on the list than documents that had all three words in them. By entering instead **+albatross +boat +fishing**, you can ensure that all three words are present in the matches you receive.

Note: *Technically, all structural elements implicitly have a + in front of them. That is, if you enter a structural element like **host:digital.com**, you don't have to put a plus because AltaVista Search assumes you intended one. Including a plus doesn't hurt anything and might make it easier for you to see what's going on.*

Excluding Specific Words and Phrases

Just as you can require particular words you want to search for, you can also exclude words that you don't want to see on the pages listed as matches to your search. Excluding words is handy if you know there is more than one way to understand the term you are searching for and you don't want to be inundated with matches that have the right term but the wrong meaning.

For example, if you wanted to find documents about the Mona Lisa that did not also talk about the Louvre museum, you would enter **"Mona Lisa" -Louvre**. AltaVista Search would return all documents that had the two words *Mona* and *Lisa* together (capitalized as you entered them), but exclude any document that also had the word *Louvre*. Similarly, **+digital audio recording -"Digital Equipment"** would look for documents that have the word *digital*, would prioritize those that also had both *audio* and *recording*, and would exclude those that talked about *Digital Equipment* (Corporation).

Inslude AltaVista Search in Your Home Page

Make AltaVista Search Your Own!

Do you use AltaVista Search often and would you like to access it even more quickly? Just build it into your own page.

Simply enter the following lines of HTML code in your personal home page. If you're not quite sure where to begin to create a personal home page, try searching for **+creating personal pages**.

```
<FORM method=GET action="http://altavista.digital.com/cgi-bin/query">
<INPUT TYPE=hidden NAME=pg VALUE=q>
<B>Search <SELECT NAME=what>
<OPTION VALUE=web SELECTED>the Web
<OPTION VALUE=news>Usenet
</SELECT>
and Display the Results <SELECT NAME=fmt>
<OPTION VALUE="" SELECTED>in Standard Form
<OPTION VALUE=c>in Compact Form
<OPTION VALUE=d>in Detailed Form
</SELECT></B><BR>
<INPUT NAME=q size=55 maxlength=200 VALUE="">
<INPUT TYPE=submit VALUE=Submit>
</FORM>
```

Remember, although you're welcome to utilize the form for your personal use with AltaVista Search, you may not use it for any commercial purpose without written permission from Digital Equipment Corporation.

Combining Elements in Your Searches

You can perform very complex searches easily by combining different terms, phrases, structural elements, and include (+) and exclude (-) flags. For instance, if you want to know how many Web pages outside of your own site have hypertext links to your site, then type **+link:yourdomainname.com -host:yourdomainname.com**. To find documents about microprocessors, but only at Intel's Web site, enter **+microprocessor* +host:intel.com**. AltaVista Search will return all documents that have the word *microprocessor* and are located at a server owned by Intel.

*T***ip:** *You can use the minus sign (-) to exclude any unwanted results from your search. For example, if you're searching for parenting tips, but you're not interested in issues involving step-children, just search for **"parenting tips" -step** and you're there.*

All the mechanisms we discussed above for creating phrases with either quotations marks or punctuation apply here as well. And you can combine several of these structural elements with one another and with ordinary words and phrases. Remember, you can include more than one of these structural elements in the same query, and they will be treated the same way as if they were individual words. For instance, **text:comet image:jupiter nasa** would look for the word *comet* in the text, the word *jupiter* in the address of a picture, and the word *nasa* anywhere in a document, then rank the combined set as usual and present it to you.

3

Advanced Search

Now that you've mastered Simple Search, you're ready to jump into Advanced Search with both feet. You'll notice that some of the features of Advanced Search are similar to the Simple Search; however, you have to work a little harder with Advanced Search to set up the query. The payoff is that you get much more control over the results.

Why did the AltaVista Search designers provide two different ways to do something very similar? Because people search differently. Simple Search, which is fully as powerful as Advanced Search, takes less thought and organization to whip out a quick search. Advanced Search is more structured and takes a little more effort to construct a good search, but you get more control over the search. That said, even the AltaVista developers normally use Simple Search, unless they particularly need to restrict the search based on dates or to precisely control the ranking of the matches.

You can think of Simple Search accepting queries in conversational language, while Advanced Search requires more precise, clinical, technical usage. Simple Search interprets your search and ranks and returns the most likely matches, while Advanced Search requires you to provide conditions for ranking and organizing your results.

Most people (at least those who aren't pretty well steeped in Boolean logic) find it easier to dash off a Simple Search. On the other hand, Advanced Search clarifies possible ambiguities (that Simple Search ignores) and returns searches based on specific parameters.

For example, in preparing for a vegetarian potluck dinner, you might inventory the refrigerator and decide to search AltaVista for all recipes that include "zucchini, squash, artichokes, and asparagus." You would probably be looking for a recipe with any one of those ingredients, rather than all of them, and are using the word "and" in the loose sense of "or." Simple Search is great for this because you can just enter a query like **+recipe and zucchini, squash, artichokes, and asparagus**—just the way you thought about it. Simple Search treats words like "and" or "or" as common English words, not commands. However, as you'll see in this chapter, if you casually include **and asparagus** in your Advanced Search, you're really specifying that you don't want to see anything that doesn't include the word "asparagus."

This chapter will begin by describing the differences between Advanced and Simple Search and helping you determine which one to use when. Next, you'll learn about the Advanced Search screen (just as you did the Simple Search screen in the last chapter). After that, you will walk through all the steps involved in setting up Advanced Searches and in using the operators and other characteristics that differentiate the two kinds of searches. Finally, you will practice setting up a fairly complex Advanced Search based on a couple of sample searches.

Why Use Advanced Search?

In many cases, the Simple Search mode can provide results that are just as good as you could get with the Advanced mode. Which mode you use is often a matter of personal style and preference. In some cases, though, the capabilities of the Advanced mode make it essential. In particular, you need it:

- to search for a word or phrase that occurs *near* (not necessarily immediately beside) another one.

- to organize long, complex queries.

- to restrict your search based on dates.

- to retrieve more than 200 matching items.

If you prefer an intuitive approach or if you don't want to take any time to learn Advanced commands, Simple Search is probably best for you. However, if you envision particularly complex queries or need to specify parameters for your search, you should use Advanced Search.

 ote: *You don't really have to master Simple Search before you tackle Advanced Search. Advanced Search isn't that difficult in itself. However, this chapter will compare Simple Search (which we assume you know) with Advanced Search (which you want to know), so if you aren't familiar with either Simple Search or with searches using* and *or* or *(similar to an electronic library card catalog), you might want to check out Chapter 2 first.*

ABOUT THE ADVANCED SEARCH PAGE

Let's start by looking at the AltaVista Advanced Search page to help familiarize you with the features. Launch your browser and connect to AltaVista (**http://altavista.digital.com**). You'll see the same Simple Search page that you used in the last chapter. Click on Advanced Search in the Navigation Bar to go to the Advanced Search screen, where you'll see the elements shown in Figure 3-1.

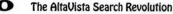

Navigation Bar

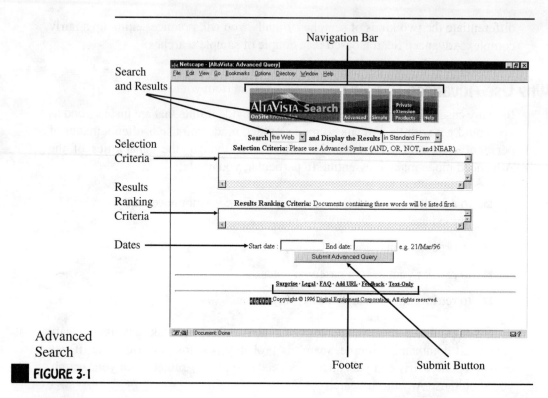

Search and Results

Selection Criteria

Results Ranking Criteria

Dates

Advanced Search

FIGURE 3-1

Footer   Submit Button

ip: *You can save yourself a step by adding a bookmark for Advanced Search right now. If you look at the URL in the location line, you'll see that it isn't one that you want to try to memorize or retype. Just add a bookmark and you can go back to the Advanced Search screen whenever you want to use Advanced Search.*

The AltaVista Search Navigation Bar at the top of the screen lets you jump to OnSite Knowledge, Advanced Search, Simple Search, Products, and Help with a click on any of the links. (This Navigation Bar is identical to the one you see when you are in Simple Search.) The remainder of the screen is slightly different from Simple Search. The following list describes the fields that you use for Advanced Search:

■ *Search and Results* is the same in Advanced Search as in Simple Search. You choose if you want to search the Web or Usenet as well as selecting the type of output—Standard, Compact, or Detailed—you'd prefer. As you will see later in this chapter, in Advanced Search you can also choose *As a Count Only* to provide only a number and not the list of results.

- *Selection Criteria* is the place where you enter the expression (including the term or terms for which you want to search and, optionally, operators).

- *Results Ranking Criteria* is the place where you enter the terms that should be ranked highest (presented first) from your results.

- *Dates* is the place where you enter an optional start and end date for your search.

- The *Submit Button* is what you click to begin the search. In the Simple Search, you could do so by pressing ENTER (in most browsers), but in Advanced Search, you must click on the Submit button.

- *Footer* information is again the same as in Simple Search, including links like Feedback, Add URL, and Text-Only.

ote: *The results you get from Advanced Searches will look just like those from Simple Searches. Please refer to Chapter 2 for more information about the format of the results.*

ABOUT THE ADVANCED SEARCH FORM

The Advanced Search Form is what you use to enter text and submit queries. It will probably take some practice to get used to exactly what to put in the Selection Criteria window and the Ranking Results window, but the examples later in this chapter should help you understand.

Essentially, the easiest way to build an Advanced Search is to add information a little at a time into one area at a time and check to see if the results are what you need. You don't have to construct a long, complex query in the Selection Criteria window; instead, enter a couple of pieces of information and add to them as necessary. By the way, if you only have one search term to enter, you would probably be better off with Simple Search, which will provide similar results with less effort on your part.

ote: *Most AltaVista searches—80 percent, actually—use only a single word. But the more information you provide in your query, the more likely you'll get the results you want.*

As you work through this chapter, you will become familiar with using the operators *and*, *or*, *not*, and *near*, as well as grouping parts of your search together with parentheses. However, all the rules mentioned in Chapter 2 for specifying capitalization, wildcards, and words and phrases remain the same here.

ote: *Did you realize that when you click on Help from the Advanced Search window, you go directly to the help screens for Advanced Search? If you do the same thing in Simple Search, you get to the Simple Search help.*

About Operators: and, or, near, and not

The words *and*, *or*, *near*, and *not* are called *operators*. (Whenever we're talking about these operators in the sense of their function in AltaVista, we'll put them in italic type.) Operators are what you use in Advanced Search to tell AltaVista how to interpret the query. For example, you can use *and* to create a query like **Pennsylvania AND 6500**. The operator *and* tells AltaVista to return all documents with *Pennsylvania* as well as with *6500*.

ip: *It really doesn't matter to AltaVista if you enter operators in uppercase or lowercase. It might, however, be easier for you to enter them in uppercase. That way you can easily see which terms you're using to search and which operators are controlling the search. Throughout this section, the examples will show operators in uppercase.*

Some people—mostly really techie types who like memorizing obscure equivalents for simple words—use shortcuts for operators. If you'd like to see how these shortcuts can save you two or three keystrokes every time you use an operator, you can use the equivalents in the table below. Many people find that these shortcuts make it easier to enter queries, but you're welcome to use them or disregard them, as you choose.

Operator	Shortcut
AND	&
OR	|
NOT	!
NEAR	~

Using the shortcut equivalents, you could either enter a search for **weather AND forecast** or **weather & forecast**. Additionally, if you want to be even more specific while using these equivalents, you could search for **weather AND (forecast NEAR extended)** or for **weather & (forecast ~ extended)**.

If you need to use a word that is also an operator as one of the search terms in a query, you must place that word in quotes. There probably won't be many instances in which you'd want to search for an operator because these words are so common that they wouldn't narrow your search very much, if at all. But sometime you might want to use *"OR"* if you are searching for something in the state of Oregon and you want to use "OR" as the abbreviation.

Using AND in Queries

Use the operator *and* to make sure that both terms are present in the resulting documents. You could enter a query like **bookshelves AND antique** to select documents with both terms. For that matter, you could keep adding *and* into your query to produce something like **bookshelves AND antique AND "for sale"**.

Using OR in Queries

Use the operator *or* in queries to get documents that match either the first or the second term you enter. The results might match both words in your query, but they don't have to. You could, for example, search for **cat OR feline**. One, but not necessarily both, of the terms would be present in the resulting documents. Again you could string several *or* operators together to get a query like **cat OR feline OR kitten**.

Using NOT in Queries

Use the operator *not* to require the opposite of the following term. For example, a search for **NOT interesting** will find all pages on the Web that do not include the term "interesting." Generally you'll use *and* with *not* to find anything matching the first term you enter that also does not contain the second term. When you search for recipes on the Web, you could enter something like **recipe AND NOT liver** to obtain recipes without liver in them. AltaVista will not accept *not* alone to join two terms, so you'll get a syntax error if you enter a query like **meal NOT liver** (although we'd tend to agree with the sentiment).

 ip: *You could search for something like **recipe OR NOT asparagus**, which would return all the documents containing the word "recipe" and all the documents in the entire Web that do not contain "asparagus." That would be an enormous number of documents, but such a search is possible and could conceivably prove useful in special cases. If you find a good use for this search, let us know and we'll include your tip in the next version of the book.*

Using NEAR in Queries

Use the operator *near* to get documents that include both of the terms you entered within ten words of each other. *Near* refers to the physical proximity of words or phrases and requires that the term preceding *near* appear within ten words of the term following *near*. For example, you might enter a query like **baby NEAR crib** or even something like **baby NEAR crib NEAR safety**. The operator *near* has no direct equivalent in Simple Search, although the proximity of terms is a factor when Simple Searches are ranked.

Note: Near *does not indicate the order of the words. In the preceding example, the word* baby *within ten words before or after* crib *would be a match.*

The *near* operator is helpful in searching for the names of people, which might appear in a wide variety of forms. While you could search for **Jimmy AND Carter** to find all documents in which both those words appear, your search would be broader than necessary—matching instances when "Jimmy" was at the beginning and "Carter" was at the end, and there was no relationship whatsoever between those names (the former belonging to some other Jimmy and the latter belonging to someone else with Carter in their name). You could also try to imagine all the possible variants and enter them all in your query as alternative phrases connected by *or* (e.g., **"James Earl (Jimmy) Carter" OR "Carter, Jimmy" OR "Jimmy Carter"**), but that would be very tedious; and if you miss a variant, you might miss the very document you need.

If you instead use *near,* you'll find just about all the matches you need. The *near* operator also gives you a shortcut for narrowing your search when you suspect that two terms will probably be near one another. For instance, if you are trying to find the home page of the Acme Company—not just one of the dozens of Web pages that Acme might have—you can search for **Acme NEAR welcome** based on the assumption that most corporate home pages include the word "welcome" and place it close to the company name. Of course, a search for **Acme NEAR coyote NEAR Wile** would be more fun because Wile E. Coyote—the roadrunner's nemesis—is mentioned on several Web pages.

3

Parentheses, Math, and Other Technical Stuff

Although you can easily string together a huge search expression with important terms and lots of operators, you should probably use parentheses to make sure that AltaVista evaluates your expression correctly. Just as you learned in your math classes, expressions are evaluated in a particular order, not just left to right. 2+3*6 does not equal 30 because the multiplication has to happen before the addition, so 2+3*6=20.

Likewise, AltaVista evaluates expressions in the following order: *near*, *not*, *and*, *or*. The phrases **marketing OR sales AND business** would root out all pages with both sales and business, and then return all of those pages plus the pages that match the word *marketing*. Generally, however, if you enter a search like this one, you'd really want all the pages with either *marketing* or *sales* and all of those pages that also contain the word *business*. Thus, you'd want to use parentheses to produce **(marketing OR sales) AND business**.

Because AltaVista evaluates expressions inside parentheses first, you know what you're getting. It's easier to remember to use parentheses all the time than to remember what gets evaluated first and to analyze the search to see if you got what you intended.

Grouping Operators and Expressions

By carefully and creatively grouping operators and expressions, you can make your queries much more effective. To keep track of what piece of the query is related to what other and to easily see the order in which operations should be performed, use parentheses to group the search expressions. If you don't do this, AltaVista will use logical rules to group the expressions for you and you might not like the results. See the "Parentheses, Math, and Other Technical Stuff" sidebar for the full scoop.

 ote: *Operations inside parentheses are performed before those outside. If you have lots of parentheses, AltaVista will start at the innermost set and work outward.*

Taking birds as an example, you could search for **robin OR oriole OR cardinal** to find documents with any of the terms. Unfortunately, you will also have some hits on things like the St. Louis Cardinals and the Baltimore Orioles. You could exclude anything with St. Louis and Baltimore or baseball, but a better way might be to group your terms together more effectively.

Because you want only information about these birds, you could search for **(robin OR oriole OR cardinal) AND bird** to make sure that you catch anything with birds. This query would find all documents with any of the three kinds of birds in addition to the word *bird*. Of course, you might need to include the technical term for the study of birds to make sure you get everything. Therefore, you might also search for **(robin OR oriole OR cardinal) AND (bird OR ornithology)**.

If you find at this point that you're still getting unwanted sports references, you could add another set of parentheses and the expressions to exclude, like **((robin OR oriole OR cardinal) AND (bird OR ornithology)) AND NOT (baseball OR football)**. This query will first find any documents with a mention of one of those three kinds of bird that also have the term *bird* or *ornithology*. It will then remove from the results list any of those documents that contain either the word *football* or *baseball*.

As you can see, you have a great deal of control over your results when you use the Advanced Search. If you take a little time to construct a query, you can almost ensure that you'll get the information you need.

Tip: *Remember that you can bookmark a search, and after you've created one of these monster search expression, you should. Just create the query you want, submit it, and then add a bookmark or add it to the hotlist in your browser. When you return to the bookmark, your browser will automatically resubmit your query and provide the latest set of results to the parameters you specified.*

The precision that Advanced Search can provide is one reason why some people prefer it to Simple Search. A quick example will show how much more effectively you can search in Advanced Search (for many things). If you want to find documents on American Indians, you would submit a query containing *American Indians* as well as *Native Americans* or even *tribe*. In Simple Search, you could simply list **"American Indians" "Native Americans" tribe**. In Advanced Search, you would have to join them together with *or* to get the same effect (i.e., **"American Indians" OR "Native Americans" OR tribe**). However, you can continue refining the Advanced Search using the operator *near* and parentheses to more accurately specify what you're looking for. The following table shows the evolution of this search.

Query	What you're doing
"American Indians"	Basic concept for which to search.
American NEAR Indian*	The wildcard (*) will ensure that plurals also show up and using *near* will broaden the range of possibilities by catching cases in which a few words separate *American* and *Indian*.
(American NEAR Indian*) OR (Native NEAR American*)	Add a second set of likely words (*Native American*) also with *near* and a wildcard. Use parentheses to link related terms. Using *or* between the parentheses ensures that either of the two elements will show up.
(American NEAR Indian*) OR (Native NEAR American*) OR tribe*	Add another single term.
(American NEAR Indian*) OR (Native NEAR American*) OR tribe* OR Indian*	Add an additional term. Now there are four possibilities, but the last one might also match terms from India, the country. The next step will fix that.
(American NEAR Indian*) OR (Native NEAR American*) OR tribe* OR (Indian* AND NOT Asia*)	The final set of parentheses includes documents that match *Indian* but do not also have the word *Asia*.

3

Troubleshooting Tips

Sometimes you will not get the kind or quality of results you expected. Check the list below for possible reasons for this and how to improve your results.

■ *If your results don't look as promising as you'd hoped,* first take a look at the word and document counts that are provided above the list of documents to check whether you entered the search syntax (*and, and not,* wildcards, parentheses, etc.) as you'd intended.

- *If you expected all of your search terms to show up in every document and they didn't,* verify that you used the operator *and*.

- *If you expected words of a phrase to appear together and they didn't,* make sure you put quotation marks around the phrase.

- *If your results seem incomplete* and you used punctuation marks or capital letters, try omitting the punctuation and changing the capital letters to lowercase.

- *If you get Syntax error (Bad Query)* and you were using complex constructions with parentheses, try checking your parentheses and make sure they match (same number of left and right). If that doesn't help, try simplifying the query and adding terms and expressions back in gradually.

- *If you're getting too many documents to sort through,* review the results from your original search and see if the documents that don't interest you have anything in common—a word, a part of their URL, or any element that you could use to exclude them from future search results by using *and not* in Advanced Search.

- *If a document you found just doesn't look like it fits with the rest,* keep in mind that the Web is constantly changing. Some people edit their pages frequently. It is possible that when the page was retrieved and indexed it would have been a match for your query, but the new version (which hasn't yet been reindexed) doesn't fit. Eventually the old information will be dropped from the index, and the new content will be indexed. But for now, you are left with a mismatch.

Restricting Your Search by Date

Advanced Search lets you limit your query to a specific range of dates by entering dates into the Start Date and End Date fields. You enter dates on the AltaVista page

3

immediately under the Results Ranking Criteria field. The dates you search by refer to the most recent revisions of Web pages—that is, the dates found in the Web documents indicating when they were most recently changed. Unfortunately, there's nothing to indicate if the whole document was overhauled on that date or if a single typo was fixed. Despite that, restricting searches by date can be very helpful when you have a rough idea of when something was placed on the Web, when you are looking for facts and comments about an event, or when you don't want to bother with Web pages you consider too old to be of use.

Although restricting searches by date can be an effective search technique, keep in mind that the date affixed to a Web page by the server is not always correct. Although most dates on Web pages are accurate, you can't completely rely on them.

Note: *Restricting searches by date is more useful in Usenet searches than in Web searches, although if you know the date or range of dates of specific Web sites, you could also effectively use date restrictions for Web searches as well. You can also use the Date fields to help search through a specific time period through many items, all of which might be important to you. For instance, you can keep your entries in the query and ranking boxes constant and vary the range of dates to see results from only a couple of weeks or months at a time.*

Entering Dates

Entering dates is easy. Whether you want to enter a start date, end date, or both, you enter dates using the form day/month/year. You must use three-letter abbreviations (from most common European languages) for months and two-character abbreviations for years. The dates you enter should follow these examples:

3/Jan/97	14/Feb/97	17/Mar/97
22/Apr/97	2/May/97	7/Jun/97
4/Jul/97	12/Aug/97	22/Sep/97
16/Oct/97	17/Nov/97	18/Dec/97

Tip: *If you are using the date fields but aren't getting the results you expect, check to make sure that your start date is before your end date and that your start date is before today's date. Trust us—we've made this mistake more than once.*

ote: *If you enter a date but omit the year, AltaVista fills in the current year. Likewise if you enter a date but omit the month and year, AltaVista will complete both the current month and year. You do have to insert at least the day if you want to search by Date.*

Ranking within Advanced Search

In Advanced Search, you can rank the results of the search by using the Results Ranking Criteria box. In Advanced Search, if you don't specify the ranking, AltaVista does not rank the matches at all and returns them in random order. So, for example, searching for **gardening AND vegetables** in Advanced Search with nothing in the Ranking field will give you lots of matching documents, in no particular order.

If you want AltaVista to put the documents in a particular order, you'll need to enter some information in the Ranking field. You could simply put the terms from the Search field in the Ranking field (without the operators). That will tell AltaVista to apply its usual ranking procedures based on those terms. The combination of terms in the Search field and the same terms in the Ranking field yields results comparable to Simple Search. In this case, adding **gardening vegetables** to the Ranking field gives more useful results.

However, if you put different terms into the Ranking field from those in the Search field, you'll be able to both rank and narrow your search at once. For example, if you put **beginner "getting started"** in the Results Ranking Criteria field (and keep **gardening AND vegetables** in the Search field), you'll get a much shorter and more precise list. AltaVista performs a second level of filtering and puts documents that contain the ranking words at the top of the list. With the Results Ranking Criteria field, just as with the search terms, the more information you provide, the more precise your results will be.

As a rule of thumb, always try several variants on your search and test your results to make sure that what you see is what you really wanted. It sometimes takes several tries to get the precise results you want, but once you have honed your search strategies, you can narrow your search more quickly in the future.

Why You Might Not Want to Rank Results

Although ranking results is handy for most queries, there are instances when you might not want to use the ranking feature. If your purpose is to gather a set of relevant but unordered information, you might choose not to rank the results. For example, if you want a list of all pages that have a hypertext link to your Web site—information in which every match is equally important—you probably would not want to rank the results. You can also use unranked searches to survey the body of knowledge on the Web about a specific topic. The main reason for choosing not to rank is to be able to view a larger number of matches.

If you use Advanced Search and choose not to rank, you can keep hitting the "Next" button at the bottom of the results page over and over again, seeing many more matches—for example, if you want a long list of Web pages that have hypertext links to your company's pages.

ote: *The reason ranked searches only return the top 200 matches is that it takes AltaVista quite a bit of time to calculate rankings. By ranking and returning only the top 200 results, you get your results more quickly and AltaVista can move on to other work. Also, the benefit to be derived from ranking more than 200 results would be minimal, because 76 percent of users only look at the first page of query results (the top 10 matches), and less than 5 percent ask for more than five screens (50 items) of results.*

About Counting Results

When AltaVista returns a list of search results, it also tells you how many times the query words appeared and in how many documents. That count is only an estimate, but sometimes reporters, graduate students, and trivia fans try to read more into such numbers than is warranted.

Remember, AltaVista is designed primarily to help people find information. The counting is secondary, existing only because it is needed for the ranking function. For that purpose, it's okay if the estimate is off by a factor of two.

During early tests in product development, AltaVista provided exact counts for all searches. There were instances in which 90 percent of AltaVista's resources were tied up counting while only 10 percent answered queries. As a result, AltaVista now approximates most searches. Basically, if the number of matches is less than 200, the count is exact. And if the number is enormous—tens of thousands to millions—it's only a rough estimate.

As soon as AltaVista determines that the number of documents to return for a given search will be large, it extrapolates the estimate from a partial result. And when AltaVista is busy, even that count may be truncated to let the system handle new queries. Because of this approach, the counts you get may vary when you repeat the same query. For instance, searching for the same word might yield a count as high as 190,000 or as low as 100,000.

In Advanced Search, you can click on the down arrow next to "in Standard Form" and select the alternative "As a Count Only." In that case, AltaVista makes its best effort to provide an exact count. But the system is always monitoring its own load, and if it decides that counting is slowing down others' searches, AltaVista will stop the exact count and provide a close estimate.

For instance, someone might be tempted to gauge the popularity of Windows 95 over time by doing a search for "Win95" at regular intervals and comparing the counts. But since variations in the count might either be random or reflect real information, there's truly no accurate method to count something like this.

BRINGING IT ALL TOGETHER: A SAMPLE ADVANCED SEARCH

Now that you've seen all the different things you can do with Advanced Search—from using operators (*and, or, near, not*) to restricting searches by date to using ranking criteria, here's an example of how to pull it all together.

Advanced Search is very useful for finding information about business. For example, many entrepreneurs need examples of business plans that were used to get funding or to clearly define a company's plans, so instructions on how to create a business plan might be useful. This section guides you through the process of setting up a thorough Advanced Search query to find business plan samples.

This example starts with a regular Advanced Search query for **"business plan" OR "marketing plan"**. Then, the word *sample* was added to the Ranking Results field to ensure that a usable specimen would be found.

Search | the Web ▼ | and Display the Results | in Standard Form ▼ |
Selection Criteria: Please use Advanced Syntax (AND, OR, NOT, and NEAR).

```
"business plan" OR "marketing plan"
```

Results Ranking Criteria: Documents containing these words will be listed first.

```
sample
```

Start date : |_____| End date: |_____| e.g. 21/Mar/96

| Submit Advanced Query |

Word count: sample:1104719

Documents 1-10 of about 2000 matching the query, best matches first.

After looking over the results, it's clear that there are no good samples of business plans in the first few matches. It's probably time to revise the search. How about expanding the query terms to include either *business* or *marketing* and the word *plan*? In other words, **(business OR marketing) AND plan**.

This search generates lots of matches, but they still seem pretty far afield. The *and* operator in the query just requires that both words appear in the document. If *near* is included, some movement occurs. In this example, the word *sample* was shifted from the ranking to the query field and the phrase *"business plan"* to the ranking field. The query now looks like **((business or marketing) NEAR plan) NEAR sample** and the ranking field like **"business plan"**.

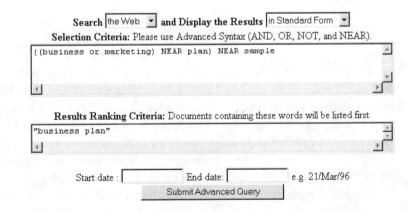

Search | the Web ▼ | and Display the Results | in Standard Form ▼ |
Selection Criteria: Please use Advanced Syntax (AND, OR, NOT, and NEAR).

```
((business or marketing) NEAR plan) NEAR sample
```

Results Ranking Criteria: Documents containing these words will be listed first.

```
"business plan"
```

Start date : |_____| End date: |_____| e.g. 21/Mar/96

| Submit Advanced Query |

Word count: business plan: about 400

Documents 1-10 of about 300 matching the query, best matches first.

A close look at the first screen of results shows a number of hits from a company at the address of **www.jianusa.com**. Their samples might be useful, but the hits from that site are keeping other possible sites from showing up in the first screen. That search can be bookmarked and then the site excluded by adding a structural element and an operator. The query string now looks like this: **(((business or marketing) NEAR plan) NEAR sample) AND NOT host:jianusa**.

A review of the first couple of screens shows exactly the results required, so this search is also bookmarked. Some of the sites might be worth following up on separately. For instance, the Small Business Administration has a number of useful sites that appear in the search. You can try adding another structural element tag requiring a host with *sba* (Small Business Administration) to the Search query field, yielding **(((business or marketing) NEAR plan) NEAR sample) AND host:sba**.

Search [the Web ▼] and Display the Results [in Standard Form ▼]
Selection Criteria: Please use Advanced Syntax (AND, OR, NOT, and NEAR).

```
(((business or marketing) NEAR plan) NEAR sample) AND host:sba
```

Results Ranking Criteria: Documents containing these words will be listed first.

```
"business plan"
```

Start date : [   ]   End date: [   ]   e.g. 21/Mar/96

[Submit Advanced Query]

Word count: business plan: about 17

Documents 1-9 of 9 matching the query, best matches first.

Because business plans are relatively timeless, no attempt was made to narrow the search with dates. On other topics, searching with dates might be a good idea. Additionally, it was not actually necessary to fine-tune the search as much as in this example. If you were willing to look through two or three pages of hits, you could have stopped enhancing the query after the first or second search. Stopping earlier probably would have yielded very similar information, but would have required looking through several more screens to see it.

However, by taking the time to really focus your search, you can save the best query and reuse it any time you want to get the latest and greatest matches.

ote: *Don't forget! You can improve your results by searching according to the structural elements text, title, link, anchor, url, host, domain, image, and applet. Just enter the element followed by a colon and the word or phrase you want. Refer back to Chapter 2 for more information about structural elements.*

Chapter 6 presents a number of further examples of how other people are using AltaVista to create effective searches. In the meantime, Chapter 4 introduces Usenet (or network news) searches to get the latest from Internet discussion groups and Chapter 5 discusses effectively providing information.

3

What's the Difference? Comparing Advanced Search with Simple Search

Although Simple and Advanced Search have some similarities, they are in fact quite different in how they handle the four operators, punctuation, and rules for words, phrases, and capitalization. This section shows you how the two search methods differ.

Operators

Three of the four Advanced Search operators—*or, and,* and *not*—have close equivalents in Simple Search. The table below presents these operators and the following section explains how the equivalents work.

Advanced Search	Simple Search
OR	Entering terms with only a space between them
AND	Placing a + before both the terms that in Advanced Search are linked by AND
NOT	Preceding a term with -

When you connect two or more words or phrases with *or* in Advanced Search, such as **Macintosh OR Mackintosh**, AltaVista processes the query as it would **Macintosh Mackintosh** in Simple Search (except that Simple Search ranks the results and Advanced Search does not). In other words, this

Advanced Search with OR is the same as entering a series of terms with no commands at all. Such a query matches all documents that contain any one of the words or phrases, but not necessarily all of them.

You cannot explicitly use the operator *or* in Simple Search. You won't get an error if you try, but it will just be interpreted as a word and then discarded because it is so common. You just need to type the important words in Simple Search. On the other hand, in Advanced Search, you cannot simply type a list of words and phrases; you must connect them with an operator such as *or.* When you connect two or more words or phrases with *and* in Advanced Search, such as **governor AND Nevada**, your query is roughly equivalent to **+governor +Nevada** in Simple Search, except that the Simple Search results will be ranked. In other words, all those words or phrases must be present in a document for it to count as a match.

When you connect two or more words or phrases with the operators *and not* in Advanced Search, such as digital **AND NOT watch**, your query is equivalent to **digital -watch** in Simple Search. In other words, the word or phrase preceded by *and not* or the minus sign must be absent for a document to count as a match.

If in Advanced Search you want to use any of the four operator command words as words rather than commands, you have to put them inside quotation marks. For instance, you might want to search for **"OR"** as an abbreviation for Oregon. In that case, you might search for **weather AND Oregon OR "OR"**.

Rules

In Advanced Search, the rules for defining words and phrases, capitalization, wildcards (*), and structure are the same as for Simple Search. But there are instances where the same expression in a query could have a different meaning in the two search modes. For instance, in Advanced Search, the symbols + and - are interpreted simply as punctuation; in Simple Search, the + and - are operators that carry special meaning for AltaVista. However, the punctuation characters &, |, !, and ~ have meaning in Advanced queries but not in Simple Search.

3

Punctuation

In Advanced and Simple Search modes, most punctuation marks serve the double function of indicating the beginning or end of a word and linking a string of words together as a phrase. However, in Advanced Search mode, parentheses and the symbols used as commands (& | ! ~) are interpreted differently. To avoid confusion, if you want to create a phrase in Advanced Search, the best way to do so is to enclose the text in quotation marks.

4

Searching Usenet
Newsgroups

In addition to using AltaVista Search Public Service to look for information on the World Wide Web (as described in Chapters 2 and 3), you can also use it to search Usenet newsgroups. *Usenet newsgroups* (sometimes called just *news* or *network news*) are simply collections of messages addressed to a group of people with common interests, rather than messages addressed to a single individual. Each of the over 16,000 newsgroups in existence has a designated subject, on any topic from books to the culture of Nepal to obscure variations of Unix. Each of the more active groups generates hundreds of postings per day. However, you can use AltaVista Search to search through all news postings over the course of a month or more and select just the messages you want to read, without having to wade through the rest of them.

Because Usenet discussion is free-form, spontaneous, and publicly available to almost everyone on the Internet, it offers a new and different type of information from what the Web offers. Newsgroups are very current and are therefore *the place* to look for reviews and reactions to a movie that just came out yesterday, or for people's reactions to the latest political crisis or product announcement or corporate acquisition.

While the Web pages of corporations often reflect the official outlook and are subject to multiple reviews, news postings by employees of those same corporations tend to be spontaneous, and normally are not reviewed by anyone other than the author (just as e-mail is not normally reviewed). So if you want the official corporate view and reliable information about product specifications and prices, look to the Web pages. However, if you want the real picture of what people say about your products and those of your competitors, look to the newsgroups.

Why should you search newsgroups using AltaVista Search? You could just read the groups you are interested in with your news reader software or with your Web browser, right? With millions of new items posted every couple of days, very few people can find the time to keep track of what is happening in more than half a dozen groups. AltaVista Search allows you to search through all the words in all the current postings in over 16,000 newsgroups and immediately read just the items you choose. Additionally, AltaVista Search allows you to easily search for specific information—like what your customers *really* think of your product—that you'd otherwise only see after wading through mountains of messages.

For example, searching for information about a specific subject could well span several different newsgroups with each focusing on a different aspect of the overall subject. With a regular news reader, you'd have to check each newsgroup. With AltaVista Search, on the other hand, you just type in your search words once and AltaVista Search finds results from all current postings in all newsgroups.

Because newsgroups are by their very nature spontaneous and unstructured, AltaVista Search does not archive postings forever. Depending on disk space and message volume, some messages will be retained as long as several weeks, while others might expire from the server in only a couple of days. After a couple of months, however, the oldest news postings certainly have expired off of the AltaVista Search server, only to be replaced by a fresh batch.

This chapter focuses on the how-tos of searching newsgroups using AltaVista Search. The first part, "How AltaVista Search Improves Newsgroups," explains what kind of information is available to you when you use AltaVista Search to search newsgroups. The next part, "Searching Newsgroups," provides you with the essentials of searching newsgroups using Simple Search. "About Newsgroup Search Results" helps you interpret the results listing, while "Newsgroup Search Structural Elements" helps you focus on key parts of messages (like subjects) instead of wading through the whole message. The next part, "Fine-Tuning Simple Usenet Searches," provides examples of how to apply what you already know about AltaVista Search Simple Search to searching newsgroups. The final parts, "Doing an Advanced Search of Usenet" and "Fine-Tuning Advanced Usenet Searches," provide—you guessed it—everything you need to know about searching Usenet using the Advanced Search.

About Newsgroups

Most Web pages today are one-way—providing static information for people to browse through. In contrast, newsgroups are interactive, allowing everyone to participate and placing no one individual or company in the role of owner or information provider. Newsgroups are where you should go if you need help or if you want to help others. They are perfect if you like to share information or make friends with people whose interests are similar to yours. Ask an appropriate question and you're likely to get a couple of dozen answers within a day or two, from people all over the world who are willing to go out of their way to help a stranger. Ask a focused group about something completely irrelevant to their discussion and you're likely to get dozens of "flames," informing you of your error.

While Web pages tend to be carefully constructed, edited, and formatted, newsgroup postings are typically informal, spontaneous messages. They resemble e-mail in length and style, but are addressed to a group rather than to an individual. The number of regular readers might be as small as a few hundred or as large as 100,000. A few groups are "moderated," which means that someone filters the postings, deciding which get included. However, most groups are wide open and welcome postings from anyone, as long as the messages are relevant to the target subject matter, consistent with the spirit of the group, and in tune with the general culture.

Note: *"In tune with the general culture" means that you should look before you leap—monitor the group for a little while to see how it works before you start posting messages.*

Except in the relatively rare moderated newsgroups, there is no editor at all. No one intervenes to polish words and sentences. No one double-checks spelling and syntax. No one, except the person who wrote it, decides whether an item should be included.

Note: *Some Usenet Newsgroups have content, often sex-related, that many people consider objectionable. AltaVista Search Public Service makes no attempt to filter, screen, or censor newsgroup content, just as your telephone company makes no attempt to dictate what you should say on the telephone. If the title of a group or a newsgroup name suggests something that might be offensive to you, do not read it.*

HOW ALTAVISTA SEARCH IMPROVES NEWSGROUPS

AltaVista Search Public Service provides complete access to newsgroups. AltaVista Search not only carries a full "feed" of over 16,000 newsgroups, but also lets you directly access each individual message among the millions posted each day. Normally, to read newsgroups you must have access to a news server, and you must know how to use your news reader software. Even then, you might find that, for a variety of reasons, your news server handles only a very limited selection of groups.

However, with newsgroup searches in AltaVista Search, you can search the full collection of newsgroups. When you click on an item, you get the full text of that article directly from AltaVista Search or—your choice—from your local news server (if it carries the group).

Searching Usenet with AltaVista Search provides several advantages over simply reading Usenet news in more traditional ways. The primary advantage is AltaVista Search's ability to help you focus on specific information. Before AltaVista Search, some Internet old-timers were ready to give up on newsgroups because there was simply too much information to keep track of and the nuggets of information were buried in too much other text. Few people have the time to scan through dozens or hundreds of messages to find really good and useful information. Now, with AltaVista Search, submitting a quick, targeted search can help you focus on the material most valuable to you—and get to it quickly, regardless of the group or groups it's posted in.

As an example, think of the benefits of being able to search for all messages that mention your company. Finding out what your customers, competitors, or business partners are saying about your company could be useful, couldn't it? Or consider using AltaVista Search to locate posts or messages by an individual or those that include a specific phrase. You can search by the author of a posting and find everything else that he or she has written to any newsgroup over the last month or so. By the way, some employers now run AltaVista Search searches for postings by potential employees, just to get an idea of where their interests or foibles lie.

*R*emember: *When a query yields good results, you can bookmark that query; the next time you click on that bookmark, you can resubmit the search and get fresh results.*

*N*ote: *AltaVista Search follows the standard practice of deleting all newsgroup messages after some period of time, typically two to four weeks. (It's increasingly common for items that have more enduring archival value to be reposted on related Web pages.)*

Finally, AltaVista Search allows you to construct a very focused search by subject and find items on that topic in dozens of different groups that you otherwise wouldn't even have known existed. This helps you discover previously unknown groups that you might want to read and participate in regularly. Likewise, when you have something to say or ask, you can quickly find newsgroups where it would be appropriate to post your remarks.

SEARCHING NEWSGROUPS

This section gives you the ins and outs of Simple Usenet Searches. You'll first learn the basic instructions about connecting (for those of you who are just jumping into the book here) and follow up with information about the specific commands and ways to tailor your search results.

To begin searching newsgroups, follow these steps:

1. Connect to the Internet.

2. Open your browser.

3. Connect to AltaVista Search by typing **http://altavista.digital.com** in the Location field. The Location field is near the top of your browser window.

4. Press ENTER.

Good. You're connected. Now you're ready to start.

When you first arrive at the AltaVista Search home page and Search Form, the drop-down menu at the left (circled in the following illustration) shows "the Web."

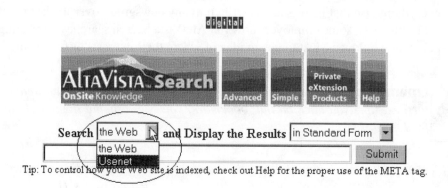

1. Click the down arrow and choose Usenet. (You don't need to change the search results from the Standard setting.)

 Note: *The Standard setting for results for Usenet searches is Compact. If you want more information about each of the postings, you'll need to change the Search Results to Detailed. Keep in mind that if you switch to the Detailed mode, you won't be able to see a set of results on a single screen as you can in Compact mode.*

2. Type **vacation** in the Search field.

3. Press ENTER or click the Submit button.

4

Almost immediately you'll see a list of thirty items that match the search terms you entered. The response is virtually instantaneous, even though you did just search through the current contents of over 16,000 newsgroups with a total of over four million separate postings.

 Note: *The basic rules for using Simple Search, discussed in Chapter 2, apply here as well.*

 Tip: *Keep in mind that Web and newsgroup searches are separate. You cannot search both with a single query. But you follow the same procedures for composing and submitting queries in both cases. So, unless you are using commands that are unique to the structure of either the Web or newsgroups, you could submit a query on the Web, leave those same terms in the query box, quickly switch to Usenet, and resubmit the query there without having to retype anything.*

ABOUT NEWSGROUP SEARCH RESULTS

The results from a Simple newsgroup search, shown in Figure 4-1, are similar to the results from a search of the Web with Compact results. The standard format of your results is Compact (details about each match are presented on one line), and the information available is slightly different from Web searches, but key information you'll need is similar.

 Note: *The menu graphic and search form are exactly as they were in Figure 2-1 in Chapter 2.*

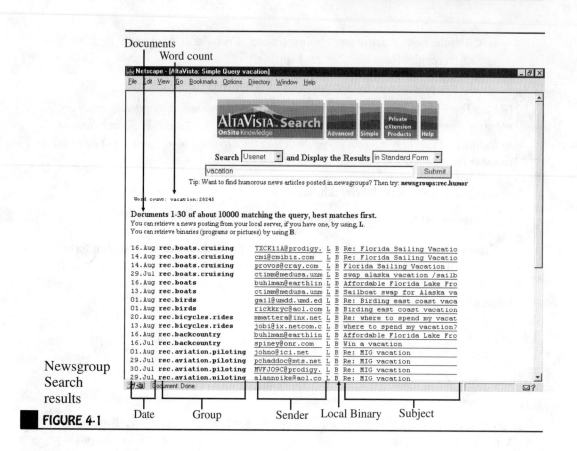

FIGURE 4-1

Remember that there is more information available than you can immediately see. You are just seeing the details compressed into one line because you used the Standard setting, providing Compact results for Usenet searches. If you can't tell whether the results are what you had hoped for from the Compact format, resubmit the search but select Detailed to see more information on what your search uncovered.

Word Count

The Word Count line tells you how many times your search term or terms were found. Additionally, if you searched for a particularly common word, the Word Count line will tell you which terms were so common that they were discarded for purposes of ranking the relevance of particular documents.

Documents

The Documents line tells you the number of documents that AltaVista Search found on your search and which ones are available on the current screen. When you first submit your search, you will have documents numbered 1-30, generally out of some much larger number of documents. AltaVista Search may also have found duplicate postings—items that were "cross-posted" to several different groups at the same time—and will report back if such duplicates were discarded.

Date

The Date column in the results area tells you the date as a number and abbreviation for the month. You'll notice that the year isn't visible. It really isn't necessary because newsgroup postings expire as they age and are deleted when they expire—in six to eight weeks, maximum.

Group

The Group column shows the newsgroup name—or part of it. Longer group names are truncated, but you'll still see enough of the name to tell if the group may be of interest to you.

Sender

The Sender column shows the e-mail address of the person who sent the message. If you click on the address (and your browser is configured correctly), you'll be able to send e-mail directly to that person from your browser.

Local (L)

The letter *L* stands for *local*. If you click on it, you will connect to your local news server (if you have one and have selected it in the setup of your browser) to read the item there. If, for example, you live in Boston and have a slow Internet connection, it would be better to connect to your local news server, rather than reading news from the AltaVista Search server in Palo Alto, California.

 emember: *When you connect to your local server, you'll leave the AltaVista Search site. To return to AltaVista Search—to check other matches or to enter a new query—use the Back button on your browser.*

ote: *If you're using the local option, you may not be able to retrieve the posting from your local server, for one of the following reasons:*

■ *Your local server may not include the newsgroup you're interested in.*

■ *Your local server's expiration policy may not be the same as AltaVista Search's.*

■ *Your local server may not yet have received the article.*

In all cases, if the local option doesn't work, you can still retrieve the posting directly from AltaVista Search.

Binary (B)

The letter *B* stands for *binary mode*. Normally, AltaVista Search will reformat the text in a newsgroup posting into HTML coding for viewing on your browser. This results in clear bold headings and pages formatted so they look more readable in your browser. However, some newsgroup postings contain encoded binary information, such as clip art files or executable programs, and the Binary option allows you to download them in a usable form, which the regular link will not provide.

Subject

The Subject column shows the subject of the posting. The subjects generally, but not always, reflect the content. Remember, sometimes people change the topic of the message without changing the subject line to correspond to what they're talking about. If you click on the subject, AltaVista search delivers the full text of the item to you immediately.

Page Numbers

Page numbers are shown in the footer of the Search Results. Most will show up as links, but the number 1 is just regular text, not a link. It shows you that you're on page 1. You can click the individual numbers to see additional pages of results, or you can click Next to move to the next page. After you've moved to one of the other pages of results, you'll have the additional choice of Prev (for previous). Note that the number of your current page is never a link, but you can always link directly to all other pages of results.

Footer

The footer information is just like that of the regular Simple Search results—it presents links to a variety of information about AltaVista Search and Digital Equipment Corporation.

 Remember: *If you click on the arrow next to Results at the top of the page, you can choose the form of the results listing. What you get as Standard in Usenet search is the abbreviated form of the information. If you want to see more detail on the matches for your search, try using Detailed.*

NEWSGROUP SEARCH STRUCTURAL ELEMENTS

Newsgroup searches can be quick and easy when you're searching for relatively rare words or phrases, and all the techniques for improving results that work for Web searches work here as well, with one exception. Here, the structural elements you search for refer to newsgroup structure rather than Web structure. These structural elements correspond to lines in the headers of newsgroup items, similar to the header lines in e-mail messages.

Table 4-1 presents a brief overview of the Newsgroup Structural Elements for reference.

from:

The structural term *from:* gives you more control over your results than you'd initially think. The amount of information contained in that line varies greatly, but in many cases it includes, in addition to the e-mail address, the full name of the poster and sometimes other identifying information, such as a nickname or employer name. Generally, you'd search for the whole or partial e-mail address, as in **from:president@whitehouse.gov**.

You could also search for **from:magna.com** to limit your search to postings by anyone with *magna.com,* for instance, as the host name of his or her mail address. A search like **from:ford.com** would limit your search to postings by employees of Ford Motor Company (posted from their corporate address), which could be quite useful if Ford is a competitor or customer of yours. Anything that might appear in the "From" line of a posting is fair game for search. You could easily search for **from:"Lee Iacocca"** and find all of his postings to newsgroups (if there are any), or combine a *from:* search with other search terms to get a more precise listing.

Element	At-a-Glance Description	How to Enter the Search Information
from:	Searches only in the *from:* field. Matches e-mail addresses and sometimes real names or company names.	from:bill@whitehouse.gov from:"Bill Clinton"
subject:	Searches news articles' subjects. You can combine this with a word or phrase.	subject:"for sale" subject:election
newsgroups:	Matches news articles posted in newsgroups with that name (or partial name). Often used in combination with other search terms.	newsgroups:rec.humor
summary:	Searches in the summary field (of articles that have summaries).	summary:invest*

Newsgroup
Structural
Elements

TABLE 4-1

subject:

The structural term *subject:* lets you search for anything that might appear in the subject line. If you are looking for information on a product called the *Gooblefitz* and would like to focus on those articles that have that as the main topic, use **subject:Gooblefitz** as a search parameter. (If you actually find something about a Gooblefitz, please e-mail the authors.)

Searching by subject line works no matter how many other words appear in the subject line and whether the term you specify is first, last, or in the middle. The element *subject:* is also a good way to track down an entire discussion on a single subject, including replies and forwards, because the subject line of a reply is typically in the form of **re:"subject name of the original posting"**.

newsgroups:

The structural element *newsgroups:* limits the search by newsgroup. You can submit a query that uses the entire name of a group, as **newsgroups:rec.arts.books**. You can also open your search to a large category of newsgroups, such as, in this example, **newsgroups:rec.** This approach can be very useful since newsgroup names are built from a series of abbreviations, separated by periods, that in their left-to-right sequence indicate a hierarchy from general to specific. (See sidebar.)

summary: and keywords:

Right now, the searching value of the two structural terms *summary:* and *keywords:* for newsgroups is minimal. These fields depend on the author's willingness and ability to provide a summary and specify keywords. The author of a newsgroup posting may, depending on software, have the option to attach a synopsis and to designate certain words as keywords, to help people with news reader software to find the posting and save time figuring out if it's something they should read. But at this time, few authors provide these organizational tidbits.

About Newsgroup Categories

The seven original newsgroup categories are:

comp	Addresses anything computer-related.
rec	Includes topics like hobbies or pastimes.
news	Deals with the Usenet news network itself.
sci	Deals with science. Surprise!
soc	Addresses a variety of social issues, often related to a particular culture.
talk	Encourages debate and expressing opinion for the fun of it.
misc	Addresses almost anything else and includes such useful groups as misc.jobs and misc.forsale.

Many other categories exist. These other categories originated in a variety of ways but are now part of the same newsgroup environment.

You can get all of these and more through AltaVista Search, but your local news server might or might not provide access to the whole collection. Some of the most common additional categories include the following:

alt	Covers every subject under the sun. These groups all bypassed the traditional newsgroup creation process for a variety of reasons.
bionet	Addresses biological sciences.
bit	Reproduces messages from some of the popular e-mail distribution lists, usually known as *listservs*.
biz	Welcomes advertising and marketing, unlike most others.
de	Covers a full range of topics, but in the German language.
fj	Covers a full range of topics, but in Japanese.
ieee	Is from and for the Institute of Electronic and Electrical Engineers.
gnu	Is for the Free Software Foundation and its GNU project.
k12	Is intended for topics about education from elementary through high school.
vmsnet	Focuses on Digital Equipment's VAX/VMS operating system.

Additionally, whole other sets of newsgroups target geographic areas, which are evident in the newsgroups' names, such as the following.

ne	New England
ba	San Francisco Bay Area
ok	Oklahoma

Note: *Often newsgroup authors submit their postings to several related groups at the same time. By sending them to more than one group, they extend their audience, making sure they reach all the people they want. Unfortunately, these cross-postings also sometimes reach many people with no interest in the topic. For this reason, you may find the same message in several newsgroups.*

How to Find Replies to Your Own Postings

If you are an active newsgroup participant, one of the problems you face is finding out when people have responded to your postings. If you post a number of different items to a number of different groups, you have to check each of those groups on a regular basis, which can be very time consuming. With AltaVista Search, there are quick and easy—if approximate—ways to use the structure of newsgroup postings to look for replies, such as searching for the subject under which you posted your messages.

If your e-mail address is huckfinn@sawyer.com and you posted a query about painting, you could do a simple search for **+painting huckfinn** to get all messages with painting, giving preference to those with your id anywhere in them. Check Chapter 6 for more precise examples of how to glean select information from newsgroups.

FINE-TUNING SIMPLE USENET SEARCHES

Aside from the different structural elements, newsgroup searches are identical to Web searches. All the same principles and practices apply. As soon as you're used to the different set of structural elements and get some practice with identifying new techniques, you'll have searching Usenet under control. This section leads you through the process of developing a few Usenet searches, as shown in the following samples.

Note: *The vast majority of the Usenet postings you'll be searching through are brief and informal messages. While some of the postings might be as long as a magazine article, that happens quite infrequently. Most of the time you'll just find brief questions and answers. You'll also find an occasional diatribe, but will rarely locate them with **diatribe** searches (if only it were that easy!).*

ALTAVISTA.. Search
OnSite Knowledge

Private
eXtension
Products

Advanced | Simple | Products | Help

Remember: *When you search by* newsgroups:, *don't be surprised if the list of newsgroups shown in the left-hand column does not match the group you entered in your query. When people post messages to multiple groups, AltaVista Search only lists one of those with the summary of matches. When you click on the item itself, you'll see the names of all of the groups to which that item was addressed.*

- **Search 1:** Suppose that your new puppy is chewing everything in sight. You could search the Web for information, but it might be better in this case to search Usenet to get people's opinions and comments on this problem. You can set AltaVista Search to search Usenet and look, for example, for **puppy training**. You'll get thousands of matches, far more than are useful. You could narrow your search down by adding *chew** and requiring all the words to be present. For example, **+puppy +training +chew*** will get you a full collection of people's opinions on the subject.

- **Search 2:** Since newsgroup information is updated continuously, repeated and careful newsgroup searches can be very important in uncovering bargains, competitor tactics, sales opportunities, and customer relations issues that need to be dealt with immediately. For instance, to find out what employees of Ford have been saying about Pentium computers in computer-related newsgroups, you could pose the query **from:ford.com newsgroups:comp pentium**.

- **Search 3:** If you would like to know what everybody but Digital employees is saying in computer-related newsgroups about Alpha computers in general and the 8400 model in particular, you could query **-from:dec.com -from:digital.com newsgroups:comp +Alpha +8400**.

- **Search 4:** On a less techie note, if you worked for one of the companies that syndicates columnists, you could search for the columnist by name to uncover copyright violations. **"Dave Barry"** is a pretty reliable infringement case to search for. If you suspect that correct attribution may not have been given as the columns work their way around the network, you could always search for key phrases from a specific column, such as the first or last sentence, to find a column without the author's name but with the same content.

- **Search 5:** What if you want to learn more about scanners? You could start your search with **scanner***, though your results might be a little too comprehensive. To include only the newsgroups that focus on scanners for PC computers, you could add to your query **scanner* +new sgroups:pc**. You should probably require that *scanner* appear, or you'll have so many postings you won't know what to do with them all. So, your search could consist of **+scanner* +newsgroups:pc**.

After scanning—so to speak—through the first few groups, you'll notice that many of the postings are from the "forsale" groups. Exclude these messages by modifying your search to: **+scanner* +newsgroups:pc -newsgroups:forsale**. Now, if you further exclude postings that deal with radio scanners and virus scanners, you'll be pretty much on target. Your final search will look like this: **+scanner* +newsgroups:pc -newsgroups:forsale -radio -virus**.

Actually, it would be a good idea to pick a less versatile word than *scanner.* If you were interested in character recognition, you could have searched for **OCR "Optical Character Recognition"**, or, for images, you could have searched for **+scan* +image**.

■ **Search 6:** Using country or regional newsgroup hierarchies can be very useful when your intention is to make physical contact with someone, for instance, buying or selling second-hand items, or when you are looking for entertainment and social activities in which you could participate in person. For instance, if you were interested in buying a vehicle in New England, you could do a search like **subject:"for sale" newsgroups:ne SUV "Sport Utility Vehicle"**.

Keeping your Newsgroup Postings from Being Found

If you have any qualms about people using AltaVista Search to find a particular newsgroup postings of yours, you can easily prevent your posting from being indexed. AltaVista Search does not index postings that contain the field: *X-No-Archive: Yes* in their headers. This field should appear on a line by itself in the header of the message, like the *from:* field. Like all header fields, upper and lowercase are equivalent for the purposes of recognizing the header.

Some users cannot, for a variety of reasons, include the header in the correct way, so AltaVista Search also recognizes *X-No-Archive: Yes* if it is found as follows:

- anywhere in the header (including embedded in another field)

- anywhere in the first few lines of the message body

- anywhere on the last line of the message

However, if you can avoid it, don't rely on this flexibility. If *X-No-Archive: Yes* isn't in the conventional place in the header, other search services might find and index your posting.

ip: *You should always assume that anything you post to newsgroups will get back to everyone you know. Postings, particularly the ones you regret as soon as you send them, have a life of their own and will probably end up where you don't want them,* X-No-Archive: Yes *or not.*

DOING AN ADVANCED SEARCH OF USENET

If you prefer an intuitive approach or if you don't want to take any time to learn Advanced commands, Simple Search is probably best for you. However, if you envision particularly complex queries or need to set some restrictions on your search, you should use Advanced Search. The operators that you use in Advanced Search are particularly useful in gleaning good information from Usenet, so Advanced Search might be a good choice if you spend a lot of time doing Usenet searches.

Just as the Simple Search of Usenet was like the Simple Search of the Web, Advanced Search of Usenet is like Advanced Search of the Web in many ways. The structural elements of your search and information you search for are the same in both simple and advanced Usenet searches, as are the formats of the results.

You should submit Advanced Usenet Searches if you want to:

■ restrict your search based on dates.

■ search for a word or phrase that occurs *near* another one.

■ organize long, complex queries.

■ retrieve more than 200 matching items.

If you need a quick review of the mechanics of Advanced Search and the logistics of using operators and the different fields available, refer to Chapter 3.

To begin doing Advanced Searches of Usenet, follow these instructions:

1. Connect to the Internet.

2. Open your browser.

3. Connect to AltaVista Search by typing **http://altavista.digital.com** in the Location field and pressing ENTER.

4. Click Advanced Search when AltaVista Search appears.

Good. You're connected. Now you're ready to start.

In the Search Form, the drop-down menu at the left (circled in the following illustration) starts out with the Web selected.

1. Click the down arrow beside Search and choose Usenet. (You don't need to change the search results from the Standard setting.)

ote: *The Standard setting for Usenet searches is Compact. If you want more information about each of the postings, you'll need to change the Search Results to Detailed. See Chapter 2 for more information about the different formats in which AltaVista Search provides your results.*

2. Type **holiday** in the Search field.

3. Click the Submit button.

Just as with Simple Search, you'll almost immediately see a list of thirty items, culled from the millions of postings to over 16,000 newsgroups. The results from an Advanced Usenet Search are just like those from the Simple Search, covered earlier in this chapter. You should see something like this:

Documents 1-30 of about 20000 matching the query, in no particular order.
You can retrieve a news posting from your local server, if you have one, by using **L**.
You can retrieve binaries (programs or pictures) by using **B**.

11.May	alt.2600	Blacque.Jacques.	L B	TIMS needed
13.May	alt.2600	Tommy@f26.n340.z	L B	Re: $250 cookie recipe from
18.May	alt.2600	marcus@telis.org	L B	Re: $250 cookie recipe from
22.May	alt.2600	jpvc@gate.net	L B	VH$ Network, Shop at Home
11.Jun	alt.2600	Gunfire@adm.mona	L B	Re: Dumb Americans Compared
11.Jun	alt.2600	Bwa@io.com	L B	Re: Dumb Americans Compared
07.Aug	alt.2600	pc93@gate.net	L B	Lost Light 15-1
13.Jul	alt.angst	thedavid@clark.n	L B	By The Way...
14.Jul	alt.angst	dfrancis@facstaf	L B	Re: By The Way...
15.Jul	alt.angst	mpa@cyberus.ca	L B	Re: By The Way...

The results from the Advanced Usenet Search look just like those from the Simple Usenet Search. See "About Usenet Search Results" earlier in this chapter for a detailed explanation of the different parts of the page.

Review of Advanced Operators

The words *and*, *or*, *near*, and *not* are called *operators*. They are what you use in Advanced Search to tell AltaVista Search how to interpret a query. For example, you use *and* to create a query like **military AND intelligence**. The operator *and* tells AltaVista Search to return all documents with *military* as well as *intelligence*.

The following table reviews the operators and their equivalents, and provides a brief explanation of each one.

Operator	Shortcut	Explanation
AND	&	Use *and* to make sure that both terms are present in the resulting documents.
OR	|	Use *or* to get documents that match either the first or the second term.
NOT	!	Use *not* to exclude something.
NEAR	~	Use *near* to get documents that include both terms within ten words of each other.

If you need to use an operator as one of the search terms in a query, you must place it in quotes. Otherwise, the operator will not be part of the search term—it will just do its *and*, *or*, *not*, or *near* job. You probably won't often want to search for an operator because the words are so common that they wouldn't narrow your search very much, if at all.

 emember: *To use Advanced Search successfully, you will have to be familiar with using* and, or, not, *and* near, *as well as grouping parts of your search together with parentheses. All the rules for specifying capitalization, wildcards, and words and phrases remain the same as they are in Simple Search. Refer back to Chapter 3 for detailed information about using Advanced Search.*

All of the Usenet structural elements discussed earlier in this chapter also apply to Advanced Usenet Searches. Remember that you can only use Usenet structural elements if you're searching through Usenet, just as you can only use Web structural elements if you're searching the Web. For example, you can specify *newsgroups:soc* for a sociology-related newsgroup when you're searching Usenet.

FINE-TUNING ADVANCED USENET SEARCHES

Most of the nuances of getting good results with your Advanced Usenet Search differ very little from those of Advanced Web Searches. If you're comfortable with the structural elements of Usenet searches that were covered earlier in this chapter and with Advanced Search in general (Chapter 3), you won't have any problem applying your knowledge to Advanced Usenet Searches.

 emember: *If you're using Advanced Usenet Search, you'll need to use operators if you have multiple words or phrases to search for. You will more easily find the messages you're looking for if you also specify Ranking Criteria for your searches.*

The ability to specify dates in Advanced Search is probably most important when you do newsgroup searches. You can easily identify the information you seek by narrowing the scope of your search based on the date. In this case, the start and end dates you enter refer to the time stamped on the article when it was first posted, just like a postmark. For example, if you put today's or yesterday's date in the Start field, your query will be restricted to the most recent articles available on AltaVista Search.

 ote: *News articles are stamped with the local time and date when they are posted. You should probably leave a one-day margin if you're looking for messages from a specific time period and it's important that you not miss any. For example, a posting from halfway around the world may have a time stamp twelve hours different from your local time, and a different date.*

Searching by date can be very helpful if you have a rough idea of when something was posted, if you are looking for facts and comments about a recent event, or if you don't want to be bothered with information you'd consider out-of-date. Here is a sample Advanced Search.

Note: *Entering a start date but leaving the end date blank will search from the start date to today's date.*

If you'd posted a message to several newsgroups about *computer performance* two weeks ago, and wanted to check to see if anyone posted a reply, you have several avenues open. You could search for **computer AND performance**, use *newsgroups:* to specify which groups, use *subject:* to indicate the title of your posting, and enter a date of two weeks ago in the Start Date field. There's not much point in searching for replies from the time before you posted the question, so you can exclude all of those dates from your search.

4

Tip: *If your original query specified either* Macintosh *or* PC, *you might put that in the Ranking Criteria field to further narrow the list of results.*

You could also use the Dates field to manage your search through many items, all of which could be important to you. For instance, researching this book required checking newsgroups for mentions of AltaVista Search. Thousands of such items have appeared since December 15, 1995, the launch date of the search service. By limiting the search for comments on AltaVista Search to a specific day, and proceeding day by day, it was possible to find thousands of comments, some of which we've included in this book's A to Z section, Chapter 6.

Tip: *If you are using the Date fields but aren't getting the results you expect, check to make sure that your start date is before your end date and that your start date is before today's date. If you enter a date but omit the year, AltaVista Search fills in the current year. Likewise, if you enter a date but omit the month and year, AltaVista Search will add the current month and year. You do have to insert at least the day if you want to search by date.*

Remember: *Newsgroup postings are periodically deleted. Don't expect to find items more than a few weeks old, although the actual length of time that AltaVista Search keeps newsgroup articles varies. For example, at the time of publication,* comp.* *groups were kept somewhat longer than* alt.* *groups, but nothing was kept longer than about two months.*

5

Providing
Information the
AltaVista Way

If you're an Internet content provider—that is, someone who creates Web pages or posts to newsgroups—you can use this chapter to investigate how to use AltaVista Search Public Service to provide information more effectively. While AltaVista Search will eventually find virtually everything on the Internet, if you're a content provider, you control potential readers' initial impressions of your site and content and should help ensure that your site makes it into your potential reader's results. You can tailor your information to take full advantage of AltaVista Search's unique capabilities, in addition to making sure that information is (or is not) found and indexed for the rest of the world to access.

In general, people who provide content on the Internet, either as Webmasters or newsgroup participants, often have an unusual perspective about searching the Internet. For them, what matters most is not finding, but rather being found, and being found in the best way. They want to make sure that their potential readers will easily find the relevant or appropriate information they've created, to ensure that their pages appear near the top of results lists, and to encourage readers to actually follow the link to their site. If you're one of these people, this chapter is for you.

In this chapter, you'll find everything you need to know about providing information effectively:

■ An explanation of how AltaVista Search finds sites and how to submit your site manually, instead of just waiting for AltaVista Search (Scooter) to find you.

■ A thorough description of AltaVista Search's indexing techniques and ways to customize your documents.

■ Complete instructions on excluding your site or pages from it.

■ Specific document design and structure tips.

■ A description of how AltaVista Search acquires news articles and how you can control the way your postings are indexed (or not indexed) by AltaVista Search.

HOW ALTAVISTA SEARCH WORKS FOR WEB PAGES

This part of the chapter briefly outlines how AltaVista Search collects and indexes Web sites and provides the necessary background for you to structure your own site for most effective inclusion in AltaVista Search. Knowing how the program finds and indexes Web pages helps you control how your pages are treated, making sure that your readers can find you and that you can find yourself.

How AltaVista Search Finds Sites

The Web—comprising tens of millions of separate documents—is dispersed on over two hundred thousand computers around the world. Capturing information from these millions of documents requires a computer program to visit each site and each page, just as a regular human user would, and retrieve all the text that is found there. These programs that automatically visit Web sites and gather information are known as "spiders" or "robots."

AltaVista Search's spider, called *Scooter*, sends out a thousand simultaneous connections to a thousand different Web addresses (Uniform Resource Locators, or "URLs"). It goes to each of those sites, submits a URL, and retrieves the complete text of the Web page. It then parses the pages and identifies other URLs mentioned, checks to see if they have already been retrieved, then goes and gets the new ones. That process continues until Scooter has reached all pages that are connected to other pages on the Internet. This technique enables Scooter to retrieve as many as four million Web pages per day.

Note: *Wouldn't all the commotion caused by Scooter retrieving pages clog up a Web site? Actually, no. To avoid such problems, Scooter pauses between retrievals from a specific site. The exact length of the pause depends on the response time of the site—when retrieving text from a slower site, Scooter will wait longer. This approach guarantees that if a particular machine is overloaded or has a slow Internet connection, Scooter will wait that much longer before returning for the second or third time.*

As remarkable as Scooter is, it does not quite retrieve everything. For example, there are some pockets of pages that link to one another but that have no connections with the rest of the Web—theses pieces of information might not be found. Additionally, there are entire private networks behind firewalls, including most corporate networks, that Scooter cannot access. Finally, Scooter does not retrieve those pages where Webmasters have indicated that they do not want to be visited by robot programs (using the Robot Exclusion Standard, described below).

A good way to understand Scooter is to think of someone using a text-only browser or of a blind person using a text-to-speech synthesizer searching the Web. Any text that's available will be understood, but images and graphics, not to mention video and sound files, will go unseen and unindexed.

Submitting Your Site

Normally, there is no need to tell AltaVista Search that you exist, that you have changed your pages, or that one of your pages has gone away. Pages are in the index not just because someone sent in directory information, but rather because they were actually visited and the full text was retrieved. However, there are a few circumstances in which you would want to submit your URL directly to AltaVista Search.

You should submit your URL manually to AltaVista Search in these situations:

■ Your site is relatively new and very few other sites have pointers to it.

■ Your site is already in the AltaVista Search index, but you recently added new pages or made significant changes to existing pages.

To make sure that users of AltaVista Search will be able to find your site and all its Web pages as soon as possible, you can submit your URL. To do this, click "Add URL" at the bottom of any AltaVista Search page. You'll see a screen similar to Figure 5-1. You just need to enter the URL for your Web site in the URL field.

AltaVista Search retrieves the page right away, indexes it quickly, adds the information to the index, and then adds your URL to the list of sites for Scooter to visit the next time out. By following the links from your home page and the subsequent links from there, Scooter will be able to find the rest of your pages.

 Note: *Scooter will also revisit existing sites and notice when pages no longer exist. They will automatically be purged from the index.*

How AltaVista Search Indexes Sites

After Scooter retrieves a site, AltaVista Search builds an index of every word in every document using custom-designed indexing software. By taking this approach

Alta Vista
Search
Add URL
Screen

FIGURE 5-1

rather than developing a directory or structured database, AltaVista Search deals with chaotic information in its natural disorganized state and doesn't try to turn the Internet into something it isn't—like a telephone book or an encyclopedia. AltaVista Search lets you find a needle in a haystack without having to rearrange the haystack first.

ote: *The same basic indexing software is used for both newsgroups and the Web, though the indices themselves are kept on separate machines. Both Simple and Advanced Search use the same index and the same indexing software.*

How AltaVista Search Ranks Sites

When you submit a Simple Search query, the results you get are a listing of ranked documents, not just a random listing of documents AltaVista Search found on the topic you submitted. This section provides information about how the program ranks sites and how you can make your site more accessible.

AltaVista Search ranks the information you receive using two elements:

■ The rarity of words you provide in the search query.

■ The location of search words in the documents.

The most important ranking factor is the rarity of words you provide in the search field. When a potential reader submits a search, AltaVista Search ranks the results based in part on how uncommon the terms are. Extremely common words (e.g., *a, and, the, Internet, computer*) are ignored for purposes of ranking because they appear in so many documents that they provide no help in establishing how relevant a given document is to your query.

ote: *On the results page, along with the word count, you see which words were "ignored."*

The next most important factor for ranking is the position within the document of the query words and phrases. AltaVista Search presumes that position within a document often indicates the relative importance of a word to the document as a whole. For example, a word in a title is generally more indicative of the content of the document as a whole than a word in the body of the text several screens deep in the document.

Specifically, AltaVista Search prioritizes according to the following rules:

■ Pages that have the target words in the HTML title and near the top of the text are ranked higher than others. This rule includes any content in <META> tags in the head of the document.

■ Pages in which the words appear near one another in the text are ranked higher than those in which the words are farther apart.

■ Pages in which the word appears twice are ranked higher than those with only one occurrence. (More than twice makes no difference.)

The indexing software looks through the documents in the index and considers every document that includes at least one of the words in the query, calculates the score for each matching document, ranks the matching documents according to score, and then generates a prioritized list of Web pages.

*N***ote:** *Because of the immense scope of the information indexed—tens of billions of words in tens of millions of documents—AltaVista Search uses approximations for ranking. Rather than determining precisely if a given word appears in 149,985, 150,003, or 150,010 different documents, AltaVista Search rounds off to 150,000—a good approximation.*

If you make marbles, you may be tempted to repeat the word *marbles* hundreds of times in your pages in the hope that anyone searching for marbles will see your page first. However, that technique won't work because of the way AltaVista Search is designed to rank pages. For purposes of ranking, AltaVista Search only counts up to two occurrences and ignores everything beyond the second instance of the word.

For AltaVista Search, it's much more important to put words that are important to you in the title of your page. And if you specialize in black marbles, be sure both those words appear together in the title in case of a two-word search or even a phrase search by someone who would make a perfect customer for you. If there is a related word that is relatively rare—like *agate,* or a brand-name—put that information in the title or in the first couple lines of text, too.

What AltaVista Search Does Not Index

As an information provider, you must ensure that AltaVista Search can index enough of your site to make sure that your potential readers can find it. Normally, AltaVista Search indexes only HTML or text formats, which seems fairly limited since many Web sites contain so much more than these basic formats. This section presents ideas that you could apply to overcome these limitations. You should pay particular attention to these if your site:

- requires registration or password-based access.
- relies heavily on images rather than text.
- relies on specialized formats (such as Acrobat and PostScript).
- uses primarily multimedia files.
- includes extremely long (over 4MB) text files.
- provides dynamic or very frequently and automatically updated content.

Registration or Password-Based Access

Some sites require registration or passwords for users to access the information. For example, some sites welcome visitors to the home page and then require them to go through some additional step, such as filling out a form, registering, or providing a password before proceeding further. Procedures like these stop Scooter in its tracks. If that's how you've established your site, only your home page will be indexed. That means that people checking AltaVista Search to get an idea of where to go for your kind of information or service may not even realize that you exist.

Heavy Use of Images

Some sites publish pages containing mostly images rather than text, or pages relying exclusively on imagemaps (clickable images) to provide navigational links to other pages. This is quite common when the layout is considered to be of primary importance. AltaVista Search can and does index pages linked through a client-side imagemap, but the older-style server-side imagemaps pose an impenetrable barrier.

Just think of Scooter as a browser without the ability to view images and you'll be fine. If readers can use your site and get the information they need without being able to see images, Scooter will be able to handle it.

Specialized Formats

Many sites use specialized formats rather than HTML or text-based formats to present information. For example, PostScript and Acrobat files are attractive and usable for many people, but do not readily lend themselves to full-text indexing by AltaVista Search or other search engines. Although there is text within the files, AltaVista Search cannot read them and people using AltaVista Search will not know that you have such rich content—all they might find is the filename. You should at the very least make your filenames clear and descriptive, or, far better, provide the plain text as a supplement to the more attractive or fancy files.

Multimedia Files

More and more, people are adding nifty effects to their Web sites, such as audio and video files. Again, these files are not automatically indexed by AltaVista Search. While there is no need to remove or reduce the number of graphics, audio, video, and other multimedia files at your site, you should

- give them clear and descriptive names.
- provide detailed descriptive text.
- provide alternative forms of the same information, if possible.

Dynamic Information

If your pages change very often—either to suit the profiles of individual users or to constantly update with the latest news, like stock quotes—these pages won't be indexed either. When AltaVista Search encounters a dynamically changing site, it only indexes the static content—for instance, the front page, help, and background pages. AltaVista Search will look at the basic text on the page, but not at anything that's automatically added to the page when your readers view it.

Additionally, pages that use "cookies" (to identify visitors when they return) in the URL will be eliminated from the index, simply because the text indexed would not match what a user would see when linking to that site through AltaVista Search. See "Excluding Pages or Sites from AltaVista Search" later in this chapter for more information about automatically keeping these pages from AltaVista Search.

Large Files

Enormous text files (4MB or over 2,000 pages of text) are also not completely indexed by AltaVista Search. Documents larger than 4MB are truncated to 4MB by Scooter when it fetches them. Then, in the current index, documents larger than 100K have everything in their first 100K indexed and only links indexed thereafter. So if you have text files larger than 100K and you want their full contents indexed, you should consider breaking them into a series of smaller files, by part or chapter. (This step will also make the files *much* easier for your readers to use.)

Controlling How AltaVista Search Indexes Your Site

Even though AltaVista Search does not index all information from all pages, you can control how AltaVista Search indexes your site. AltaVista Search provides you with a few quick-fix alternatives that help you direct readers to your Web site. This section outlines ways that you can help potential readers find you through AltaVista Search as well as other tips that might make your pages more usable in general.

As an information provider, you have several tools in your arsenal to ensure that your potential readers can find your pages. There are several areas you can control that will have a significant effect on how AltaVista Search indexes your site (see Figure 5-2):

- HTML document title
- abstract or description
- date
- keywords
- content

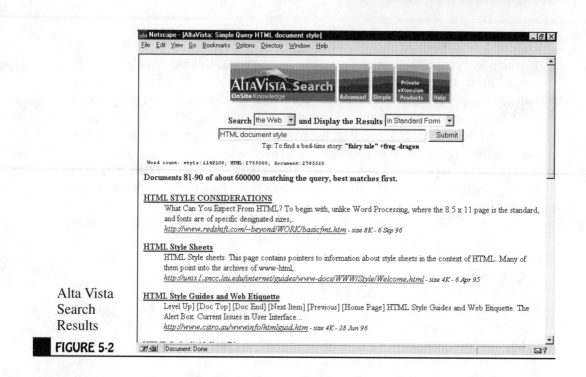

Alta Vista
Search
Results

FIGURE 5-2

ote: *There are no tricks that allow you, as Webmaster, to ensure that your pages appear on the top of results lists. The best you can do is to be clear, direct, accurate, and complete in all your descriptions, using the words that people who want to find you are most likely to use and understand.*

HTML Document Title

HTML document titles are the first thing your potential reader will notice in the list of search results. Titles are not the headings that appear in large, bold type at the top of Web pages, but rather, they are the text lodged between <TITLE> and </TITLE> in the HTML document source.

If you're counting on readers finding you through AltaVista Search, you need to pay particular attention to the HTML titles for two reasons. First, the HTML title is usually the piece of information people use to decide whether to visit—or not to visit—your Web site. Because of this, you should make sure that you include it and that it clearly describes the page.

Second, the HTML title is important because words in the title are given priority for ranking purposes. If there are words that people would naturally search for when they want to find a site like yours, make sure those words are in the title. In this context, accuracy and completeness are extremely important.

HTML document titles appear in the source of a page between the tags <TITLE> and </TITLE>. If you're using a browser like Netscape, you will see the title of a page only at the very top of your Netscape window, in the title bar.

> *N***ote:** *Some content providers use existing pages as templates when creating new ones and, unwittingly forget to give the new page a new title. That is why results lists from AltaVista Search sometimes show several different entries with the same title, titles that don't seem to be accurate, or pages that don't have any title at all.*

Abstract

The second element that an AltaVista Search user is likely to notice in a results list is the abstract or description. The abstract or description simply provides some data about what information your site contains. In many cases, AltaVista Search just uses the first few lines of your HTML document for the abstract. If those lines are (or could be) appropriately descriptive, great! However, if the first few lines are not particularly descriptive or if you want to present a more global description of your site, you can tell AltaVista Search exactly what you want the abstract to say.

To specify what you want the abstract to say, include the META tag between the document <HEAD> tags. For example, suppose you're the Webmaster for ACME Corporation and one of your pages starts like this:

```
<HTML>
<HEAD>
<TITLE>Developments at ACME Corporation Innovative Devices</TITLE>
</HEAD>
<BODY>
<H1>ACME Corporation Innovative Devices Information</H1>
```

You can add a META tag to the document head with a brief document abstract, using the format <META name="description" content="ACME Research and Development efforts continue to be successful.">

The top of your document would then look like:

```
<HTML>
<HEAD>
<TITLE>Developments at ACME Corporation Innovative Devices</TITLE>
<META name="description" content="ACME Research and Development
efforts continue to be successful.">
</HEAD>
<BODY>
<H1>ACME Corporation Innovative Devices Information</H1>
```

After Scooter revisits your site, AltaVista Search will return your new description with the URL when people search for information contained at your site.

Dates

The third item that your potential readers will see within search results is the date that the page was last modified. This date reflects the last time that particular page was modified, not necessarily the date other information in the site was last modified. This date might be misleading for your potential readers because you might have, in fact, updated some pages in your site but not the particular page that AltaVista Search retrieved.

No matter how good your content may be, if people see a date like May 15, 1994, prominently displayed at AltaVista Search, they'll often presume the site is inactive and the information is obsolete. The date is also important to Scooter, which only looks for new material. If for any reason, the version number or date of a page has not changed, Scooter will not revisit it, and new material there will go unindexed. Therefore, when updating pages in your site, you need to be sure that pages related to the one you're updating also reflect a new revision date.

Additionally, you have to make sure that your server is properly configured to send out the correct date and time. AltaVista Search has found files dating from the first half of the 20th century, as well as some from the 21st. Presumably these file dates result from server error, rather than a time warp.

Keywords

Another aspect you should consider to help your pages be more accessible are keywords. *Keywords*—any particularly descriptive terms—augment the content of your HTML documents by adding other terms through which your potential readers could find you. Keywords are not directly visible to your potential readers, but they do help ensure that your potential readers will find your site when they need to.

The content alone of your document, taken out of the context of the rest of your site, might not necessarily be sufficient for potential readers to track you down. For example, as the Webmaster for ACME Corporation, you might have placed all your company's press releases online. Whenever people visit your site, they can select a link for the latest information about the company and that's worked well so far. However, the phrase "press release" probably never appears on any of those pages. In other words, someone searching for **"ACME Company" AND "press release"** might find nothing.

There are two possible remedies for that kind of situation. First, you can simply edit the text to add the necessary words and phrases. Second, you can designate keywords that may or may not appear in the text by using the META tag. This section covers adding keywords using the META tag.

Adding keywords to a document simply requires editing the HTML code and adding information within the HTML <HEAD></HEAD> tag, as in the following example. Before AltaVista Search, the top of an HTML document on your site might have looked like:

```
<HTML>
<HEAD>
<TITLE>Developments at ACME Corporation Innovative Devices</TITLE>
</HEAD>
<BODY>
<H1>ACME Corporation Innovative Devices Information</H1>
```

For instance, to indicate that a particular document is a press release, create a META tag with the following information:

```
<META name="keywords" content="press release">
```

If you need to add additional keywords, you can throw them in as well.

```
<META name="keywords" content="press release Wile Road Runner failure
still trying">
```

The top of your HTML document would then look like:

```
<HTML>
<HEAD>
<TITLE>Developments at ACME Corporation Innovative Devices</TITLE>
<META name="keywords" content="press release Wile Road Runner failure
still trying">
</HEAD>
<BODY>
<H1>ACME Corporation Innovative Devices Information</H1>
```

An AltaVista Search search will match any of the words listed, even though a visitor to that page would not see the META tag, and might not see those words anywhere in the text. Someone searching for +"ACME" +release would not have a problem finding you. Additionally, searches for **ACME road runner Wile** would now also get your page as a match.

When deciding which words are "key" for you, take advantage of unique terms associated with your company and its products. You should use typographically unique trademarks, model numbers, and particularly descriptive or unusual names whenever possible.

Note: *There's no need to attempt to load your document with appropriate terms by using comments tags (<COMMENT></COMMENT> or <!-- -->) in the header or the body of the text. AltaVista Search deliberately does not index information in comment tags so your notes to yourself remain your own.*

As an additional example, if you are developing a site selling stereo equipment, you could add keywords like *high-fidelity*, *music*, *stereo*, *quality*, *component*, *speakers*, and the like to your documents. Consider any and all keywords and phrases that might reasonably occur to people looking for the kind of information you provide and add those words to your documents.

EXCLUDING PAGES OR SITES FROM ALTAVISTA SEARCH

Because AltaVista Search searches and indexes the entire Web, it could eventually find any Web page that is connected to the main body of the Web through even one hypertext link. Even if no links lead directly to the page, if the URL is known and submitted by anyone to AltaVista Search, the information will be available to anyone on the Web. Because any information you have on a Web site could potentially be found by AltaVista Search, you might consider specifically excluding sensitive pages from AltaVista Search.

Why Exclude?

Documents or entire sites might be excluded from AltaVista Search for a number of reasons. First, you might want to exclude your site while it's still being constructed. Because your site represents you or your company, it's important that the content and structure are in place and accurate before making it available to the world, particularly through an accidental release into the world's largest Internet search engine.

Second, you might want to exclude some pages from AltaVista Search to try to maintain some control over the context of the user's experience. You could allow pages that can serve as entry points to be indexed, and block other pages that might be confusing if accessed directly. For example, if you're running a contest with a three-step procedure to enter, you might want to block steps two and three from AltaVista Search so readers would have to start at the first step.

Third, you might want to exclude pages that only specific people should access. For example, you might exclude pages that are still under construction or that are being tested. You can provide the address to the testers or the people within your organization, but you wouldn't want them indexed on AltaVista Search.

Fourth, you might want to control which parts of your site are indexed and which are not. For instance, you may have pages that you would like to make available on the Web for the convenience of those who need them, but would prefer not to broadly publicize. You might, for example, want to make usage logs available without making it particularly easy for everyone on the Internet to retrieve that information.

 ote: *Don't assume that if there is no hypertext link from any Web page to some test or "confidential" page of yours that no one can find it. Any documents on a public Web server are at least potentially available to everyone on the Web. In fact, some Web server software has a "directory indexing feature" that lets Scooter and other robots see the entire contents of a directory, and, therefore, find and pick up files that have no links to them—pages you might consider work in process or junk. If you have any files that you would prefer that the public not see but that you must keep on a Web site, you should check your server's configuration and make sure it isn't making that information available to the world.*

The following section will tell you how to direct AltaVista Search not to index part or all of your site.

How to Exclude Pages or Sites

If you do have reason to exclude pages or sites, you can keep them out of AltaVista Search, and it's easier than you might think. AltaVista Search adheres to the Robots Exclusion Standard, which is basically an Internet honor system that specifies how robots and spiders are supposed to behave. This standard makes it easy for you to block spiders or robots from indexing your entire site, from finding particular directories, or from looking at particular files. If you're sure you want to keep parts of your site from being indexed, here's how.

Set up a file named ROBOTS.TXT on your Web server in the main (top level) directory of your Web server. This file should contain a list of the directories and files that you want to deny access to.

For instance, the file in the following example would exclude all spiders (*) from three directories (cgi-bin/sources, access_stats, and cafeteria/lunch_menus).

```
User-agent: *
Disallow: /cgi-bin/sources
Disallow: /access_stats
Disallow: /cafeteria/lunch_menus/
```

Any URL matching one of these patterns will be ignored by robots, like Scooter, that abide by the Standard. Of course, this file won't help at all if you get a disobedient robot, but that's life. So to speak.

DESIGNING YOUR SITE

Because users can come and go as they please, the structure of a Web site should be cohesive enough to hold readers' attention and to lead them through a controlled sequence of choices. Many—probably most—Web sites are organized hierarchically, with the home page as the top element, providing text links to the next level, which in turn provides links to the next level. Such a structure can make it easy for a user who comes in by the front door (or home page) to navigate smoothly around the Web site.

Before AltaVista Search, it was reasonable to assume that people navigating to and through a Web site would start with the home page and then follow through this hierarchy. But with AltaVista Search, every indexed page is equally likely to be found. AltaVista Search users are likely to bypass your home page and arrive directly at any of the pages deep in your carefully constructed directory structure. Therefore, you can no longer presume that the user has followed a certain predefined path to get to any one of your pages. So as an information provider, you should keep some additional concepts in mind when creating for this new environment:

- Provide logical and clearly labeled navigational links. Terms like "next page" and "previous page" aren't nearly as useful as links labeled by content, such as "Acme Corporation's Mission Statement."

- Clearly state the purpose of each page within the page itself. You cannot assume your reader will gain the context from other pages at your site—they might not even see other pages at your site.

- Provide links back to the main page of the site from each page in the site, in addition to information about the page maintainer and contact information.

- Look at the full text of your pages, not just the titles and descriptions. Remember, AltaVista Search indexes information from the entire page, not just from titles and descriptions.

- Make sure that each and every page can be understood by people who cannot see pictures. All graphics should have text alternatives for AltaVista Search to find, and all words should be able to stand on their own, without graphics or multimedia files.

When you're creating Web pages, try to imagine the ways in which potential visitors to your site are likely to search. Varying your writing style by using synonyms rather than repeating the same word numerous times will not only make your text more readable, but will also increase the likelihood that people will find it.

 emember: *You also can put an AltaVista Search query box right on your Web page, for the convenience of your users. The brief code that you need to do that is available at the AltaVista Search site. Simply save it and paste it into your Web page document. The simplest way to do that is to click on "FAQ" on the bottom of the AltaVista Search page. You'll see a section that provides code that you can just copy and use on your page. The result will be the AltaVista Search submission form, without the AltaVista Search graphics. People can enter their queries from the context of your site and get answers back from AltaVista Search.*

USEFUL TECHNIQUES FOR WEBMASTERS

One of the biggest challenges for a Webmaster is just keeping up with everything happening in a site. As pages and links come and go (often without notification or warning), keeping track of all the pages and how they relate can be an imposing task. The following tips and techniques will help you, as a Webmaster or information provider, use AltaVista Search to do your job more effectively.

Keeping Private Information Private

If you work for a corporation as a Webmaster, you are probably partially responsible for making sure that information that should be not public isn't available through your site. However, you also probably don't create all the pages on the site, nor do you have time to read all those pages carefully. Following is a solution that will help you keep private information from going public.

One of the first things you should do is conduct a query for documents at your site that contain any corporate information security markings. For instance, you might try the following:

```
host:yourdomain.com "company confidential" "proprietary" "top secret"
"internal use only"
```

Hopefully, a document with such warning labels wouldn't get posted on your site in the first place. But if and when such a mistake is made, you will want to know about it right away. Just bookmark that query and click on that bookmark regularly.

Similarly, as you learn of other sensitive projects and topics, create a query for those terms, bookmark the query, and use that bookmark regularly too. You might have a simple search query like the following:

```
url:yourdomain.com "Project X" "Customer X" "Acme Road Runner Cannon"
```

The same approach applies to any sensitive information at your site.

Taking Inventory of Links

Because your readers might enter your site at any page within the site, you should pay special attention to the hypertext links on all your pages, making sure that they provide good navigational clues and information about the rest of your site. You can use AltaVista Search to do a quick inventory of the internal links at your site. For instance, you can submit a query for links and URLs at your domain name, like this:

```
+link:yourdomainname +url:yourdomainname
```

The results of this example give you a list of pages with hypertext links that connect pages within your site. This list of results will provide the information you need to see which pages link to other pages, and which do not. For example, if you find a number of pages that don't include a link to your home page, you might need to look into rewriting some of the pages so people who just find those pages can also find your home page.

Keeping Up with Links to and from Your Site

AltaVista Search also allows you to check what other Web sites and pages have hypertext links to your pages, and what particular pages they are linking to. Again, you can submit a query for links and URLs at your domain name, like this:

```
+link:yourdomainname -url:yourdomainname
```

The results of this query give you a list of all Web pages outside of your Web site that point to pages at your site. If there are less than 200 such pages, you can see them all with this Simple Search query by using the "Next" link at the bottom of the page to see successive screens of results.

emember: *If there are more than 200 pages and you want to capture information about lots of them, use the following line Advanced Search (leaving the Ranking box empty):* link:yourdomainname AND NOT url:yourdomainname

Check the context in which these pages point to you and whether they point to your home page or other specific pages at your site.

ip: *You can also use AltaVista Search to find other sites that are related to your business and might be of value to your audience but who are not competitors. You might then arrange for reciprocal links with the best of them, especially those that complement the material on your own pages.*

Fixing Broken Links

As a Webmaster or information provider, there are two kinds of broken links you need to check for and fix:

- links *from* your site
- links *to* your site

AltaVista Search is particularly handy for helping you maintain links to and from your site in two situations. First, if you discover that one of the links from your site to another one no longer works, you can use AltaVista Search to track down the new address. Just set up a query for any information that you know about this link—content, filename, or anything else.

ote: *If you see in the logs for your site that people have been trying to reach nonexistent pages at your site, note the wrong address and use AltaVista Search to track down the Web page with the mistake. For instance,* link:yourdomainname/wrongaddress.html *will return a list of all Web pages that have the URL* yourdomainname/wrongaddress.html *embedded as a hypertext link.*

Second, if you have to reorganize part of your Web site or move to a new service provider, you can use AltaVista Search to find every page on the Internet that linked to the old pages or old site. (Then, of course, you have to contact everyone who linked to you and tell them about the new address, but you knew that!)

The query **link:oldaddress** will provide you with a list of every Web page (including your own) which has links to a Web page at the URL "oldaddress".

emember: *Keep in mind that when you make changes in your pages, the results are not immediately visible at AltaVista Search. Only after Scooter has visited your site again will the changes affect the contents of the AltaVista Search index.*

Overall Site Inventory

Since people will frequently access pages in your site from somewhere on the Internet (as opposed to from your home page), you should occasionally take a look at how your pages look when they're accessed individually.

In general, you should inventory your site for the information that appears with AltaVista Search results, as follows:

- HTML title

- abstract (the default is the first words in your document)

- date last modified

You should apply all of this information to *every* page in your site.

You can use AltaVista Search to help you inventory your Web site in two ways. First, you can use it to obtain a complete list of the pages at your site. If the domain name of your Web site is *acme.com*, the query

```
host:acme.com
```

will return a list of the pages at your site.

emember: *If you have less than 200 pages, then Simple Search will suffice to provide a complete list. If more than 200, use Advanced Search, leaving the Ranking box blank, so you can get many more of them.*

Such a results list can show you where you've overlooked things—for instance, using the same title for several different pages. The date on each entry can also show you which pages are old and may need to be updated.

Second, you can use AltaVista Search to find pages that shouldn't be there—versions of pages that aren't yet supposed to be public and that you thought there weren't any links to. If you find one of those, you can do another search to see where the link (or leak, in an information sense) is coming from. If the file is called *problem.html,* you'd search for

```
link:acme.com/problem.html
```

That query should return any and all pages that link to your page named *problem.html.* You can then take steps to remove that link, rename the file you don't want people to see, or just move it back to your local system and keep it off the server until it is ready to be seen.

HOW ALTAVISTA SEARCH FINDS NEWS ARTICLES

AltaVista Search finds Usenet (or network news) articles differently from how it finds Web site URLs. To find Web site URLs, AltaVista Search sends Scooter out to roam the Internet. With Usenet articles, AltaVista Search has the articles delivered right to the door, just like the difference between going to the grocery store or having the mail delivered at your home.

Usenet articles traverse the Internet by being forwarded from server to server across the Internet—the news server at AltaVista Search receives the full "feed" of 16,000+ newsgroups. The AltaVista Search news server maintains and indexes all current newsgroup articles, and, on request, serves the full text of these articles to users. Because new articles appear and old articles expire all the time, the news server at AltaVista Search is in fact quite busy, even though the total index of Usenet articles is much smaller than the Web index.

EXCLUDING NEWS ARTICLES FROM ALTAVISTA SEARCH

If you have any qualms about people finding a newsgroup postings of yours, you can exclude the article, just as you can exclude information in Web sites. All you have to do is enter a command—*X-No-Archive: Yes*—in the header of your message to ensure that AltaVista Search will not index it.

The following steps will prevent your newsgroup posting from being archived by AltaVista Search:

1. As you create your posting, include a line like the following at the very top of the message (skipping no lines).

```
X-No-Archive: yes
```

2. Skip a couple of blank lines, and then continue creating your posting.

AltaVista Search does not index any postings that contain the field *X-No-Archive: Yes* in the header. This field is meant to be on a line by itself in the header of the message, like the *From:* field (or the keyword or summary fields from the previous examples). However, because some users cannot include the header in the standard way, AltaVista Search also recognizes this command if it is found anywhere in the header, anywhere in the first few lines of the message body, or anywhere in the last line of the message.

Keep in mind that, even with *X-No-Archive: Yes* in your document, many people will be able to find your article on the Internet and it will probably exist, in one place or another, for years. If you post an article in Usenet, it's entirely possible that it will resurface at the least opportune time. If you have information that you really don't want to make public, don't post it to Usenet.

Using AltaVista Search for Searches of Your Site

After you have completed cleaning up your site and you feel good about how all your pages appear on an AltaVista Search match list, you might want to add a link to your home page that is a bookmark of a query for useful subsets of your pages. In other words, the anchor might read "Quick index of all pages about ophthalmology at this Web site," and the hyperlink would be the URL of an AltaVista Search search for

```
+url:yourdomain.com +ophthalmology
```

Keep in mind that when you do this, the user "leaves" your site and connects to AltaVista Search. But the results list that automatically appears (without the user having to fill in a query box) is a set of choices, all of which are your site.

5

6

Using the
AltaVista Search
A to Z Reference

The AltaVista Search A to Z Reference offers a collection of sample searches, examples of real-world searches, and a number of tips to make your searches more effective and successful. The Reference is intended to help you generate ideas on how to search and what techniques to use. Secondarily, it provides a broad idea of the range of topics available through AltaVista Search. Although it doesn't attempt to show everything—or even a significant proportion of everything—on the Internet or in newsgroups, it provides a representative sample of the diversity of information you can easily find, demonstrates techniques you can use to create your own effective searches, and shows how other people use AltaVista Search.

INFORMATION IN THE REFERENCE

The A to Z Reference provides an alphabetical collection of successful and effective AltaVista Search searches and a compendium of information that people have found using AltaVista Search. The items in the Reference are based on notes that AltaVista Search users have volunteered as well as some of the most popular topics and categories of information AltaVista Search has uncovered. As you thumb through, you'll see everything from acquaintances to colleges to medical information to sports, and you'll learn to use AltaVista Search to find the information you most want to locate.

The A to Z Reference provides something better than a complete or comprehensive listing of information on the Internet or in the newsgroups. In lieu of a reference of what's been found, consider the A to Z Reference chapter an encyclopedia of *how* to find information. When you look under a given letter, you'll find categories of information, sample searches, explanations of searching techniques, and even personal stories from other AltaVista Search users about their experiences.

If you'll pardon the cliché, the A to Z reference should teach you to fish on the Internet, rather than giving you fish. Frankly, the shelf-life of an Internet fish isn't so long—better to get some that is fresh. That is, all printed catalogs of Internet resources tend to become dated quickly. More information is added to the Internet every day, and a large amount of the existing information is updated regularly. So, if you refer to a printed reference, it won't include the latest information or even the newest places to look for it. This environment of constant change makes the A to Z Reference even more useful because it provides strategies on how to search and how to hone in on the information you really need.

A TO Z REFERENCE ORGANIZATION

The A to Z Reference provides an alphabetical listing of select, interesting categories and searches. Within the Reference, information is broken out by letters, just as the index of this book is divided into letters. Under each letter, you'll find several topics, chosen because they were inherently interesting or provided a good example of unexpected ways to search, or because someone told the AltaVista Search developers about their positive experience searching for that topic.

Each topic contains information about relatively obvious applications, such as searching for recipes containing *apples* (Simple Search **+recipe +apple**). Additionally, they offer further suggestions, such as finding recipes to use up the apples you have on hand, even though you don't have any cinnamon or sugar (Simple Search **+recipe +apple -cinnamon -sugar,** which yields about 4,000 hits and an unknown number of servings). In some of the search samples, you'll find cross-references to other search topics within the A to Z Reference. These cross-references not only will give you additional search ideas, but also will help show you just how "webbed" Internet information really is.

Also, throughout the Reference, you'll find boxes containing actual user stories. These anecdotes show how other AltaVista Search users like yourself have been able to apply AltaVista searches to their own informational needs. As you read through these, you're likely to see several searching techniques that you could use for your particular informational needs, and even strategies for uncovering information in ways, and on topics, you hadn't previously thought of.

WHY SHOULD I USE THE A TO Z REFERENCE?

If you've already read Chapters 2 through 4, you've undoubtedly learned how to successfully search in AltaVista Search. You can now search for appropriate terms, review the list of results, browse through the titles, and find your way to the information you need. However, as Mark Twain noted, "the difference between the right word and almost the right word is the difference between lightning and lightning bug." This section will provide examples, anecdotes, and guidance to help you immediately identify your personal lightning bug.

Seeing successful searches, for example, on marketing plans or women's rights may help you improve your own searches for entirely different information. Possibly you hadn't even dreamed of searching for some particular snippet of data, or you'd tried to find something but overlooked one key issue. The samples and examples throughout this section will help you ease into improving your own searching techniques and build on the fundamentals you mastered in the previous chapters of this book. AltaVista Search is a powerful tool that you can use in unique ways to unearth information about almost anything. We've structured the A to Z Reference both to show you how others have used it and to give you ideas on how to apply its capabilities to your own needs.

Just one more note—some of the more obscure information on the Internet might well go unnoticed without the benefit of being able to search through AltaVista Search. Let your imagination run wild when trying the program. It works.

HOW SHOULD I USE THE A TO Z REFERENCE?

Start by browsing through the Reference just to see the topics and read the user stories. If something catches your eye, read it. That'll be the easiest and most enjoyable way to dive in. The Reference wasn't designed necessarily to be read cover to cover, although you'd learn the most that way. After you're familiar with the content and have flagged a few interesting items, go back and reread those, possibly while sitting in front of the computer and trying some of the examples out with your own search topics.

Don't feel any obligation to try every example or to work sequentially through the text. Many of the examples are likely to be appealing while others will make you wonder where some people find their free time. Think of the examples as sample how-tos, not sample what-tos. And remember, AltaVista Search is an index of the content of the Web and Usenet newsgroups—if there is a topic you want to know more about, AltaVista Search will find where the information resides and bring it back to you.

A TO Z REFERENCE CONVENTIONS

The A to Z Reference consistently uses some simple typographical conventions to make it easier for you to spot the information you want. Throughout this section, the actual search query you'd type is shown

```
on a line by itself, like this.
```

The reference information itself will be the main flow of text, broken up with alphabetical dividers and headings indicating each category. All of the user stories and anecdotes will be in boxes, located near the topic they're related to. Some of the user stories have been edited for length or paraphrased, but all reflect the essence of comments about AltaVista Search.

A

acquaintances

Suppose you're trying to track down an old friend or someone who owes you money. A good place to start is with an Advanced Search for the first and last names. For example, if you're looking for Albert Einstein, search for:

```
Albert NEAR Einstein
```

on both Usenet and the Web. If that doesn't bring up anything useful (perhaps your friend doesn't have a Web site and doesn't post to Usenet), search out:

```
"white page*"
```

and try some of the dedicated White Pages services. These services are similar to your local phone book, but are not comprehensive.

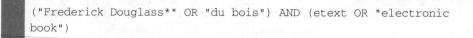

African-American history and literature

Suppose you want to put together an anthology of African-American history and literature in electronic form to distribute to your class. You are specifically interested in works by Frederick Douglass and W. E. B. Du Bois. You could do an Advanced Search for:

```
("Frederick Douglass*" OR "du bois") AND (etext OR "electronic
book")
```

You could focus the search even more, for example, by limiting the search to organizations that make electronic texts available over the Internet. If you're familiar with Project Gutenberg, you might add the name of the organization to the ranking box, like this:

```
Gutenberg
```

Now Project Gutenberg's index appears at the top of the list, and many of the other items are pointers straight to specific works that are available for free from Gutenberg online.

In Search of African Philosophy

In a comment about AltaVista Search, Jesse wrote:

I am always trying to get faculty [at my university] to use the Internet. Recently a colleague came in and told me he was interested in finding some information for his philosophy course. However, he said he doubted there would be anything on African philosophy. He was surprised to find hundreds of hits and ran off to get a disk to download several articles.

Jesse Silverglate

---

annual reports

Need to check up on the status of a company? Need to figure out if you should unload that stock you inherited? Pick a company and search away for **+"annual report"** and the **company name**, for example:

```
+"annual report" +"Digital Equipment"
```

or:

```
"earnings report" +"the company"
```

These searches give you information about the specific company as well as the reports they publish on the Web. If you're looking for more current information, try a Usenet search for:

```
+newsgroups:invest
```

or, to be a little more specific, search for **+newsgroups:invest +companyname**, as in:

```
+newsgroups:invest +IBM
```

In Search of Answers

In reference to finding postings and sending replies by e-mail, Ken writes:

Why not just set up a search with AltaVista? I find it rather impolite when people say "please reply by e-mail," even if I am not replying to them.
  For example, this page:

  *http://altavista.digital.com/cgi-bin/query?pg=q&what=news&fmt=.&q
      ="Running+time+of+C+programs"*

will give you this whole thread (unless anyone has the "x-no-archive=yes" header).
  If I have a really important question to ask, I tend to do a double-check with AltaVista.

                                                              Ken Nicolson

anonymity

The generally impersonal nature of computer networks coupled with the ease with which people can anonymously post messages has led to all kinds of interesting discussions that you can find through a Usenet or Web search on:

```
anonymity
```

This search provides you with all sorts of discussions about the pros and cons of anonymity on the Internet—interesting, not to mention a very hot topic.

In Search of Answers

In reference to a question on a newsgroup, Dave wrote:

No. I'm not gonna go through that again. This is the dozenth time I've written about this, and AltaVista came up with 50 or so posts with "mailto" and "subject" in the last three months. Did you look there?

> *http://altavista.digital.com/*
> *http://altavista.digital.com/cgi-bin/query?pg=q&what=*
> *news&fmt=.&q=%2Bmailto+%2Bsubject*

Dave Salovesh

---

art (images)

If you're interested in finding information on art (like images, pictures, or paintings), AltaVista Search is the place to look. Because of the vast amount of information on this subject available on the Internet, entering common terms like *images, art,* or *paintings* won't be too useful—these searches result in thousands of hits that would take forever to wade through.

Instead, you should narrow your search, for example, by the specific artist, like this:

```
+pictures Escher
```

or, depending on your taste:

```
+pictures Dali
```

or even:

```
+pictures "Van Gogh"
```

If you're looking for information on a type of art or a specific art period, you could try:

```
+pictures impressioni*
```

or:

```
+pictures +renaissance
```

In Search of Astronomy

In a comment about AltaVista Search, Deane wrote:

My father is interested in astrophysics and astronomy, and wanted some information on a particular star called Betelgeuse. When I searched JPL's and NASA's home page, I couldn't find anything. Next step was to search using Yahoo and WebCrawler, and they didn't find anything.

Then I decided to use AltaVista, and on the first try you found it. Now if I have to find something on the Internet, I go straight to AltaVista for it.

Deane D. Davis

B

baseball cards

"Take me out to the ball game . . ." Well, AltaVista Search can't take you to the ball game, but it can help you find that rare baseball card you've been looking for. Suppose you want to add the Ty Cobb baseball card to your collection. You could search newsgroups by entering:

```
+"Ty Cobb" +card* +"for sale"
```

This search gives you several listings of cards and places to buy and sell originals as well as reprints. You can get more specific, for instance, trying to track down the extremely rare card from his rookie year by entering:

```
+"Ty Cobb" +card* +"for sale" +rookie
```

With this search you'll find information on the card, its condition, and the price.

basketball

For all you basketball fans out there, AltaVista Search can find loads of information about it for you. You can do a general search on the topic, like:

```
basketball
```

Doing this Simple Search provides you with a wide variety of information, ranging from team status to scores to most valuable players. However, if you've entered a bar bet with your basketball buddies, you might want to hone your search a bit and find out the latest scoop on the team standings. For instance, you could enter the following Simple Search:

```
basketball handicapping
```

Also, searching for teams by name is generally productive, as in:

```
"Chicago Bulls"
```

Or you could search for officially sanctioned sites by entering:

```
basketball official
```

This search gives you not only the officially sanctioned sites, but also information on official basketball rules. If you don't want the basketball rules included, you could enter:

```
basketball official -rules
```

Or if you only want information on official basketball rules, you could enter:

```
basketball official +rules
```

Finally, if you're into collecting basketball memorabilia, you could do a Usenet search to link up with other collectors, as in:

```
newsgroups:rec.collecting.sport.basketball
```

beekeeping

If buying your honey some honey isn't enough, you could always grow your own—more fun than a barrel of ... er ... bees, we guess. Just a Simple Web Search for:

```
beekeeping
```

should get you started. On the other hand, you might try:

`bee sting`

to find everything from treatment for bee stings to using bee stings therapeutically.

bicycling

A search for:

`bicycling`

not only provides links to information about alternative transportation and columns about races, but also a number of other informational links. You can even find out just how people decided to perch on top of these two-wheeled contraptions by searching for:

`bicycle history`

for a full history, including some nifty pictures.

biochemistry

You can use AltaVista Search to find out the very latest information about a rapidly evolving topic. For example, suppose you are researching the details of the protein folding process. You'd like to determine if it is predictable and, hopefully, controllable. You have a hunch that the mathematics of chaos theory could be a useful tool here. You could first search the Web for:

`"protein folding" chaos`

Or you could refine the search even more by doing an Advanced Search to limit the topic by date. Remember, if you're looking for the latest and greatest information on a topic, you could try using the same query to search Usenet newsgroups, which often provide you with the most recent information available on a topic.

blind

Suppose you're looking for information on text-to-voice converters, which make it possible for the blind to navigate the Internet and "read" electronic texts. But graphical user interfaces—Windows in particular—threaten to lock them out. Hence many people are very concerned about and involved in efforts to make Windows applications accessible to the blind. For updates on what is happening in that area, search both the Web and newsgroups for:

```
+blind +Windows
```

Or suppose you have a blind friend who enjoys knitting and you would like to buy her a gift. You could do a search of the Web using:

```
+knitting +braille
```

and find a variety of resources for blind knitters, including a book in braille from the National Braille Press.

brewing

Thinking about brewing your own? Try reading up on different opinions and ideas. Do a general Usenet search for:

```
newsgroups:brewing
```

or:

```
newsgroups:tea
```

If brewing your own beer or tea just hasn't been quite as successful as you'd hoped, you might look for:

```
newsgroups:brewing recipe
```

or:

```
newsgroups:brewing troubleshooting
```

and find specific brewing ideas. Alternatively, you could head over to the Web side
of things and do a quick search on:

```
zymurgy
```

business

You can't just search for *business* because that word is so common it is ignored.
However, phrases that include the word *business* are still a good way to go. For
example, try:

```
"business strategies"
```

or:

```
"business plan" +"how to"
```

if you're trying to learn how to write a business plan. Also, the U.S. Small Business
Administration (SBA) has all kinds of good information that you'll find by adding
+*host:sba* to your search, as in:

```
"business plan" +host:sba
```

Or suppose you're in the market for a new computer and want to find out the Better Business Bureau record of the business from which you want to make a purchase. All you'd do is enter:

```
"better business bureau"
```

Using this search string, you can find lots of Better Business Bureau sites that can help answer your questions. Or better yet, add the name of the region or community, like this:

```
"better business bureau" +Tulsa
```

You can even find out what other people have said about the company or institution of your choice by searching for the *company name +host:angry.org,* as in:

```
"ABC Computers and Parts" +host:angry.org
```

C

canine

There's all sorts of information to be found by doing a Web search for:

```
canine
```

You'll find information from canine breeds to training to housebreaking. Or, you could even find information on specific canine topics, like:

```
canine genetic diseases
```

which you might want to check out before you buy that cute puppy in the window.

caning furniture

That old chair not holding up very well? Need to replace the cane on the seat?

```
caning furniture
```

gets you there. You find all sorts of businesses that can help you with your caning needs. Or you could limit the search to just your area, using:

```
caning furniture +Houston
```

cars

Your old heap just leave you stranded again? Spring for a new one! You can use AltaVista Search to find the latest information about buying cars—repair history, buying guidelines, and on and on and on.

Besides the obvious Simple Usenet Searches for:

```
cars automobiles
```

specifically targeted searches can be really useful. If you're seeking buying advice, turn to the AltaVista Advanced Search and put in the selection criteria:

```
(car OR automobile) AND buying
```

and the ranking criteria:

```
used
```

Of course, if you want information about new cars, substitute *new* in the ranking criteria. Likewise, substitute the make or model if you'd like to pull up information about that particular car. Switching over to the Web searches within AltaVista Search and putting *buying guide* into the ranking criteria field can also help. Note that you can substitute *repair** in the ranking criteria after you decide it'd be easier to fix it than to buy a new one.

Of course, you'll still need to sell the old heap. You could place ads in local papers and post to classified ad sites on the Web and to newsgroups. But if at all possible, you'd like to make a very quick sale; you'd like to find someone right away who is looking for the very thing you have to sell. You could try an Advanced Search of newsgroups, as here:

```
(wanted OR need) AND ((VW OR Volkswagen) AND Jetta)
```

Or you could try the same search on the Web. Toward the top of the list is a home page for the "Jetta GLX (Vento VR6)," which has a "For Sale ... or Want to Buy" section—perfect.

CD-ROM development

Suppose you have an idea for an interactive CD-ROM designed for kids. A friend suggests that you get in touch with an animator, Derek Lamb. You know nothing about the CD-ROM business, and don't know who this "Derek Lamb" character is. All you have to do is do a Simple Search of the Web:

```
+animator* "CD-ROM" +"Derek Lamb"
```

Or you can broaden this search a bit by just searching for the animator's name, like this:

```
"Derek Lamb"
```

TaDaaaa! Among other information, this search results in a directory of animators, where you can get the street address and phone number of their companies.

chemistry

Searching for chemistry information at any level? No problem; just tune into Usenet and try:

```
chemistry
```

but be sure to specify additional information, like *reactions, physical,* or *journal.* Otherwise, the random information that uses the word *chemistry* might overwhelm you.

Likewise, the Web contains a wealth of chemistry information for all needs. Try:

```
chemistry compounds
```

or:

```
nuclear reactions
```

Or if you're experimenting with human chemistry, try:

```
chemistry love
```

chess

If you are looking for a chess teacher for yourself or your child, just use Simple Search and enter all the related words:

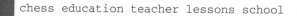

```
chess education teacher lessons school
```

You get about 200,000 responses, some of which look useful, but there are far too many to wade through. To focus more closely, try the likely phrases:

```
"chess teacher" "chess school"
```

With this search string, you'll get far fewer but more useful results. Or you could even leave the same query in the box and switch to Usenet to find related newsgroup articles, as follows:

```
newsgroups:chess teacher school
```

You'll get thousands of responses, but the top ten or so include useful discussions about chess education and particular teachers and schools. Just what you're looking for!

You can even use AltaVista Search to find out the name of a chess opening you have never seen before—simply type the moves and search on both the Web and in the newsgroups, and chances are great that if that sequence has been played often before, some of the postings include its "official" name. For instance, enter:

```
e4 c5 Nf3 d6 d4 c5xd4 c5:d4 Nxd4 N:d4
```

Because of variations in notation you need to enter both "x" and ":" for capture moves.

Keep in mind that while this only works for games that use the English abbreviations for pieces in their notation (such as "N" for knight), that represents the vast majority of games on the Internet. Also, note that since you are not specifying the order in which the moves are played, you would also find games in which the move order is transposed. In any case, this technique is quite valuable for studying an opening, researching annotating a game, or finding games similar to one that you played so you can look at alternative lines.

child development

Yes, AltaVista Search can even help answer your questions about child development. Wondering what solid food is best to start your baby on? Want to know why your baby drools so much—or more likely, when it's going to stop? Curious about when your child's babbles will turn into real words? If you're just looking for general information about child development, try:

```
"child development" process
```

Using this search string, you'll find lots of information on this subject. However, you'll probably have better luck with something more specific, such as:

```
"child development" premature
```

or focusing on specific issues, such as:

```
language development children
```

clip art

If you need some clip art to spruce up your Web site or that newsletter you got drafted into doing (you didn't *volunteer* to do this, did you?), try:

```
clipart -host:gewis
```

By the way, the *-host:gewis* excludes a site that generates a lot of matches but relatively few useful files.

If you're interested in only the *free* clipart, try:

```
clipart -host:gewis free
```

Remember that just because you find it on the Internet doesn't mean it's yours to use. Be sure when you're pilfering a nifty clip that it's really out there for you to take. See the copyright section for more search ideas.

In Search of Coconut Oil

In response to a question about finding sources to buy coconut oil,
Chuck wrote:

My normal advice is: Try using AltaVista's Advanced Search by first going to

   http://altavista.digital.com

   *Then click on Advanced Search, read the help, bookmark the page. You
can then use AND OR NEAR NOT and nested parentheses and quoted
strings with some wildcards.*
   The results of a search for "coconut oil" & order & popcorn
   Word count: coconut oil: about 2000

Chuck Demas

colleges (and universities)

So, you say you want to go to (or back to) college? And you say you've visited every bookstore in town only to find those huge books that list a bazillion colleges, supposedly to help you find the college of your dreams? Yeah, right. AltaVista Search can help!

If you already know the name of the college you want to attend, you can just enter the name, like this:

```
"Washington University"
```

or:

```
"Oklahoma State University"
```

If you only know the general area in which you want to live and need information on the colleges in that region, you could enter a search like this:

```
+Seattle colleges universities
```

This search gives you colleges and universities in the—you guessed it—Seattle, Washington, area. If you enter a search like:

```
+Portland colleges universities
```

you'll get search results from Portland, Maine, and Portland, Oregon. You could refine even further by entering, for example:

```
+Portland Oregon colleges universities
```

comic books

If baseball cards aren't your bag, you could search for the collectible of your choice. If it's comic books, you can search the Web to find pages put together by fans of the same series as you, or you can search the newsgroups for particular back issues to fill out your collection. For example, search the Web for:

```
+marvel +2099
```

and you find hundreds of Web pages dealing with Marvel Comics' 2099 series. (There is no need to include the word *comic* in your search, since *marvel* is enough to specify what you want.

You can also search newsgroups, using:

```
+marvel +2099 +"for sale"
```

and find hundreds of recent postings listing issues in that series that are for sale. To narrow the search even more, try Advanced Search and enter the numbers of the exact issue(s) you want to buy, like this:

```
marvel AND (X-nation OR Xnation) AND (2 OR 10 OR 15)
```

If you don't find what you want this time, bookmark the search and try again later. Sometimes the information or issues aren't yet available on the Internet.

In Search of Computers

In a comment about AltaVista Search, Mike wrote:

I really appreciate DEC creating AltaVista. I feel I could give you one "success" story a week about how AltaVista has helped me do my job more efficiently. I find I use AltaVista at least once a day and I'm frequently amazed at the results. Case in point—we have an old HP plotter that we are trying to connect to a Macintosh. We were having trouble finding the pinouts for the cable until I logged in to AltaVista and typed:

> *plotter Macintosh cable*

After days of frustration, AltaVista gave me the answer in seconds—outstanding!

Mike Honeycutt

---

contests

Want to enter some contests? No problem! Either on the Web or on Usenet, search for:

```
contest
```

or:

```
contest entry
```

Doing an Advanced Search and restricting the range of dates to the last few days might help identify the contests before everyone else has entered and won.

cooking

And you thought regular cookbooks had loads of recipes . . . wait until you use AltaVista Search to look for them! For the constantly changing Usenet recipes, search for:

```
newsgroups:recipes
```

If you want something specific, try, for example:

```
newsgroups:recipes bisque
```

or:

```
newsgroups:recipes chicken
```

If you're interested in getting a broader perspective than just recipes, try:

```
newsgroups:baking
```

or:

```
newsgroups:cooking
```

and throw in the items that you want to cook.

```
newsgroups:cooking oysters
```

Switching over to the Web side of things gives a world of recipes, but you'll want to have an idea of what to cook first. Entering:

```
recipe +chicken tomato* pepper
```

or some such is a good way to clean out the refrigerator. If you just can't live without that airline food, try:

```
cookbook "American Airlines"
```

If you're a vegetarian or have specific food preferences, you could create a search and bookmark it for later, as in an Advanced Web Search for:

```
NOT (mushrooms OR oysters OR liver or "brussels sprouts") AND
```

then just put the food you do want to eat at the end whenever you run the search.

copyright issues

AltaVista Search can help you do some legal research! For example, you can find out about copyright laws, what constitutes infringement, and what to do if someone infringes on your copyright. You could try a broad search, like:

```
copyright
```

This search query results in bunches of hits—probably too many to be manageable. To limit your search on this topic, you could add words to *copyright* in the query field, like this:

```
copyright law
```

This search gives you specifics on how many of the sites on the Internet infringe on other peoples' rights. Or for more information about infringement, try:

```
+copyright infringement
```

For a broader perspective, there's always:

```
"intellectual property"
```

D

dance

Looking for a weekend pastime or an after-school activity for your kids? Try dance!
You could start with a broad search, like:

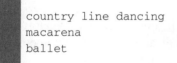

```
dance
```

to see a wide variety of information on dance. However, a quick search for:

```
country line dancing
macarena
ballet
```

or:

```
dance +instruction
```

would get your toes tapping with information about each of these as well as
information on where you can take lessons. You can also find information on more
rare types of dance, such as:

```
dance celtic
```

if you're researching historical dances, or even:

```
dance chicken
```

if you're looking for information about the infamous "chicken dance" as seen at local Oktoberfests.

In Search of Dance School

In response to someone looking for the London School of Contemporary Dance, Victor wrote:

You didn't search very hard. This took me literally less than a minute with AltaVista (http://altavista.digital.com/).
Search for **London School Contemporary Dance**. *It's at:*

http://www.ecna.org/placeds/lcds.html

Victor Eijkhout

daycare

Yes, AltaVista Search can even help you find a spot for your tot! From choosing to using, just search the Web for:

```
daycare
```

and you'll find useful information on how to select a daycare provider and how to help your little one adjust. Also, you could add your location if you're looking for a specific provider in your area, as in:

```
daycare +Dallas
```

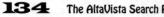

diet/lowfat references

In addition to the neat cooking ideas and recipes you can find with AltaVista Search (see "cooking" in this chapter), you can also find good diet and lowfat references. For example, you can do a Usenet search for:

```
low*fat +recipe
```

This search yields some pretty handy lowfat recipes, while:

```
cholesterol
```

leads to broader discussions, including information about cholesterol in food as well as its effects in humans. Over on the Web, you can find more information about a lowfat diet, eating well, and exercise. For starters, try:

```
"good health"
```

donations

Many people want to give to a good cause, but it's often hard to tell the difference between a good cause and a scam. AltaVista Search can't answer that question, but it can point you to some causes that happily take your money. Try a search for:

```
charity non-profit
```

or just the cause that you're interested in, such as:

```
"American Heart Association"
```

drums

Tap-ity, tap-ity, tap. You can find all sorts of information about drums on the Web, just by entering:

 `drum*`

This general search gives you everything from drum lines, drums (to play in a band), drums (to beat in the wilderness), to drummer figurines. If you're looking for more specific information, try entering, for example, specific types of drums, like this:

 `timpani`

or:

 `marching snare`

Entering these same searches in Usenet can also provide interesting information about drums. You can find all the opinions and advice you want, even information on tuning marching snares ("tight" is the word on the street).

Also, you can search for drum-related topics, like:

 `"Green Drummer"`

which leads you to a newsletter from an environmental organization. Also:

 `rhythm -"rhythm method"`

might be useful if you march to your own drummer.

E

education

AltaVista Search allows you to search for a huge range of education-related topics. For example, suppose you believe that your second grader is gifted and you want to find a private school that will give her the opportunity to develop to her fullest. You need a school that is within commuting distance of Boston. All you have to do is search the Web with:

```
+"gifted program*" +"private school*" +Boston
```

Or suppose, while channel surfing on TV, you accidentally came upon the end of an educational program on the Hubble space telescope. You notice that there's supplemental information on the Web but didn't catch the URL. You can still find the information on the Web by entering a Simple Search, such as:

```
Hubble PBS
```

You'll not only be able to reference the supplemental information that the TV program mentioned, but you'll also find a schedule for broadcast of the other programs in the series, an online teacher's guide, opportunities for students to interact with scientists, and dramatic space photos that you can download.

emergency planning

Just in case you were wondering whether your company or community is prepared for emergencies, you can check out other emergency preparedness plans, guidelines for planning, and similar information with a Web search for:

```
emergency planning
```

Or if you're interested in helping a nearby town struck by disaster, you can search for:

```
disaster recovery
```

and find out ways you can help.

In Search of the Empire State Building

In response to a question about a B-25 bomber crashing into the Empire State Building, John wrote:

14 people died in this crash on July 28, 1945. There are quite a few sites on the Web that talk about this—just do an AltaVista search on "b-25" and "empire state" Here's just one of the sites with a picture of the NY Times from that day:

http://www.westbank.org/~Calender/Disgal/planes/empire.html

John Powell

environment

Suppose you are concerned about the environment and in particular about the pollutants discharged from industry in your community. For starters, you'd like to know what the U.S. Environmental Protection Agency and others have to say about safe levels of contaminants—say copper—in drinking water. All you have to do is enter an Advanced Search, such as:

```
(EPA OR Environmental Protection Agency) AND ((wastewater OR
"waste water") OR discharge) AND copper
```

ergonomics

Spending so much time surfing the Net that your hands hurt? Try:

```
ergonomics "carpal tunnel" RSI
```

This search gives you links to information on carpal tunnel syndrome (also called Repetitive Stress Injury or RSI) as well as information on how to diagnose it, find help for it, and continue to work with it. After you've read up on it, try:

```
ergonomic office furniture
```

for information on office furniture that can help prevent RSI disorders and help improve your work environment.

The same search over on the Usenet side is worth trying, as is:

```
newsgroups:human-factors
```

which delves into a number of ergonomics-related issues.

espresso (or cappuccino)

Well, you want to keep going but just gotta have a pick-me-up? The daily grind got you down? Try a search for:

```
espresso cappuccino
```

This Simple Search gives you information about espresso and cappuccino, the different kinds, and the trends. If you want to do more than just read about it, try adding your location to the end, as in:

```
espresso cappuccino +Dayton
```

(Actually, this works better if you live in Seattle than in Dayton, but AltaVista Search serves you the information that's out there, nonetheless.)

Switch over to the Usenet side of AltaVista Search and try a search on:

```
espresso
```

for some discussion. Or:

```
newsgroups:coffee
```

broadens the scoop ... er, scope.

In Search of Employee Relations

In a comment about AltaVista Search, Ethan wrote:

This afternoon, I lost [my] Web tool AltaVista [through technical difficulties]. There was just no way I could access my favorite search engine/database. But I didn't realize until three hours later just how valuable AV is. I am in the process of writing my 4th book, and desperately need information on "minor details" and some citations on employee relations. I finally had to try other search engines, and not once did I find the references I was after. Only AV can find the obscure... To make a long story short, I have never "missed" something as much as I missed AltaVista. I was at a total loss. Thank heavens it's back. It was a definite Eureka! experience!

Ethan Winning

---

exercise

If you've discovered that exercise is more effective if you actually *do* it (rather than watch it on TV), then you might benefit from the information you can find using AltaVista Search. For starters, try:

```
exercise health fitness -balance
```

The *-balance* eliminates matches from one particular site that's interesting but tends to obscure other relevant sites.

Good for you for getting out there and exercising, but—ouch!—you say you've overdone it? Try:

```
sports medicine
```

to find information on common sports injuries, prevention of injuries, and remedies. If you find that you need to call in the big guns, search for:

```
MEDLINE
```

(yes, use all caps), which gives you the MEDLINE medical database. Or check out "medical" in this chapter for more information.

F

fast food

If you're interested in finding out just how bad for you that quick snack on the road was, try a search for the nutritional analysis of the food, as in:

```
+"nutrition* information" +McDonald*
```

With this search, you'll find all sorts of information on calories and fat, even some information on healthy choices.

fish

If you've decided that the only pet you'd ever want is silent, clean, and doesn't require walks or litter boxes, try a fish. If you're just getting into it, start on the cheap with a Usenet search for:

```
aquarium "for sale"
```

Again, add the location if you'd like, as in:

```
aquarium "for sale" "des moines"
```

You'll probably need some information about how to go about it (there's more to it than just throwing fish in the sink), so try a Web search for:

```
aquarium "getting started"
```

This search provides you with an assortment of information on selecting equipment, feeding fish, and buying fish, just to name a few. Of course, if fish as pets aren't your cup of tea, check out "cooking" in this chapter for other ideas.

flying

If you're interested in the history of flight, you should try a search for:

```
flight history
```

For reasons yet unclear, to stick exclusively with manned people-type flight, you might need to search for:

```
flight history -title:duck
```

so the aboriginal ducks don't obstruct the view. A plain search for flight history brings up quite a few matches with information about aboriginal ducks, which aren't really relevant to a more traditional interpretation of the history of flight.

foreign language and culture

Need to keep up with your foreign language? Just focus your searches on the country of your choice. For example, to see only German Web sites, add **+domain:de** to the search of your choice. For example:

```
netzwerk +domain:de
```

With this search (yes, technolog*ie* is correct—*de* is the German domain), you'll find lots of information from Germany. Because AltaVista Search covers the whole Internet, just by typing in the search string in the foreign language you'll generally get the information and language you want.

forest fires

If you want to learn more about forest fires, their causes, and how forest management practices affect them, try a Web or Usenet search for:

```
forest management "forest fire"
```

Of course, if you're going camping or hiking anytime soon, you might brush up on:

```
preventing "forest fires"
```

Or a Web search for:

```
forest fire simulation
```

lets you interactively experiment with some of the factors in forest fires without ever lighting a match. Exciting!

Also, take a look at search ideas under "forestry" in this chapter.

forestry

Suppose you're doing a research project on forestry—or even considering it as a major in college. AltaVista Search can help! For starters, search the Web for:

```
forestry
```

This Simple Search produces numerous hits, including information from university programs to environmental issues to fire prevention. Or if you want lively discussions on this topic, do a Usenet search on *forestry*. This search quickly brings up spirited debates on environmental and political aspects of forestry.

Or check out other search ideas under "forest fires" or "colleges" in this chapter.

Frisbee™

If your poor Frisbee is in retirement (or your dog has used it as a chew toy), get some fresh ideas by searching the Web, like this:

```
frisbee "flying disk*" +games
```

This search gives you several choices for disk games, although no apparent ways to discourage the dog. Or if you're young, energetic, and fearless, try:

```
"ultimate frisbee"
```

which is kind of a combination of rugby, American football, and soccer. Actually, just watching ultimate Frisbee can be fun, so check into the games even if you're not likely to risk broken bones.

G

gambling

If you're off to Vegas or just off to the local Bingo hut, you might first try searching AltaVista for:

```
gambling
```

Doing this Simple Search provides you with information on gambling regulations, locations, resorts, lotteries, and the like. For an optimistic yet ironic look at gambling, try:

```
gambling winnings
```

This search string provides you with predictable strategies to increase your winnings (no guarantees, though) as well as loads of tax forms and tax links. If you're not likely to come up with anything for the tax man, try:

```
+gambling +"average loss"
```

Or if you've just come back from Vegas or the local Bingo hut, you might try a search for:

```
"credit counseling"
```

games

The Web is full of information about games, including:

```
board games
```

or:

```
interactive games
```

These searches give you gobs of information on games for both you and your kids. You can find out what games are available, where to get them, and how to play them well. If you're looking for specific hints or tricks, the name of the game is probably the best search string. For example, entering:

```
scrabble
```

gives you information on everything from computerized versions of the Scrabble® game to tips to programs that can help you make those last three letters fit. By the way, many if not most computer games have ways of jumping ahead to the next level or of beating the system (like a virtual card up your sleeve). Try:

```
+cheat +code
```

for general information, or:

```
+cheat +code +thegameofyourchoice
```

to see if someone's posted the trick. You can, of course, also try these searches in Usenet.

See "chess" in this chapter for more game-related search ideas.

In Search of Games

In a comment about AltaVista Search, David wrote:

I was playing around with my Rubik's cube and had forgotten an important pattern. Thinking someone may have a solution on the Web, I looked around with Yahoo! to no avail. I then tried AltaVista, and there was a solutions page as the second item listed. I have found many weird things with AltaVista that I couldn't find with any other tool. Things like an old friend, a song title from the lyrics, and a satellite tracking program, all were found easily with your index.

David Skirmont

gardening

The available information on gardening is growing like weeds out there on the Web. You can search for general information by entering:

```
gardening
```

Doing this Simple Search, you'll find all sorts of information about gardening, ranging from the *Old Farmer's Almanac 1996 Gardener's Companion* to how to ensure environmentally-friendly gardening. Depending on your specific needs, you can narrow your search results in any number of ways. For example, if you want to find out how to control those pesky bugs that have eaten your tomato crop, you could try:

```
gardening +pesticides
```

With this search, you'll find lots of information on pesticides, organic pesticides, and even hydroponics. Or if you don't seem to have that green thumb, you could just do a search for gardening tips, like this:

```
gardening +tips
```

With this search, you'll find gardening tips for all sorts of plants from around the world. You can find out how to keep Peter Cottontail from eating your carrots and even find out what plants would grow best in your area.

Suppose you want to create a backyard pond where frogs can frolic in the lily pads. You'll need to find out both how to create the pond and how to start the vegetation in it. A good place to begin would be:

```
gardening +planning pond
```

Other Simple Searches can also provide you with focused garden information. Try:

```
+gardening +shows "flower and garden"
```

for information on flower and garden shows, or:

```
+gardening +hydroponic
```

for specific information on hydroponic gardening, such as tips, CD-ROMS, supplies, and mailing lists.

In Search of Games

In reference to a question about codes for a Star Wars computer game, Kevin wrote:

A good way to look up codes is to use AltaVista. It lets you search through the newsgroups and most of the time the code has been posted once.
    I found the code you were looking for by searching on "32x star wars code."

Kevin McGill

genealogy

For starters, you can search for your family name and the word *genealogy* to see if someone on the Web is systematically recording information about your family. Do this by entering a Simple Search such as:

```
+Ray +genealogy
```

Or if family tradition indicates that you might be descended from an historical figure, such as Pocahontas, you might want to track down and verify the connection. All you have to do is a Simple Search of the Web:

```
+Pocahontas +genealogy
```

The results of this search give you a good starting place.

In Search of Genealogy

In a comment about AltaVista Search, George wrote:

My main interest in the Internet is genealogy. I use AltaVista on a daily basis to scan for the surnames I am researching. I set the Advanced page to search the Usenet and then look for "genealogy and xxxx" substituting a surname for xxxx. It works well for all my surnames except Price. That one comes up with too many false hits to use.

George B. Whaley

---

geography

Suppose you're trying to do a research paper on a geography-related topic but can't decide on a specific angle. Let AltaVista Search help narrow your ideas! For starters, you can do a broad search, such as:

```
geography
```

This search provides you with data on a huge range of geography-related topics, such as physical and cultural geography, geographical anomalies, and historical geographical sites. Now suppose you've narrowed your topic to maps and geography. You can take a look around by searching for Internet map viewers, like this:

```
geography map viewer
```

or:

```
PARC Map Viewer
```

Either of these searches provides links to online geographic maps that allow you to zoom in on specified regions, cities, or towns. You can even access the information that was used to create the maps by searching for:

```
GIS geographic information system
```

Also, you can search Usenet for:

```
gis faq
```

and find out how these cool maps work, or search for:

```
geoscience gis faq
```

for related geographical information.

getting started

With what, you ask? Almost anything. Try a Usenet search for:

```
"getting started"
```

and just start browsing. You'll find tips and tricks oriented to the beginner in almost every subject under the sun. If you have specific interests, however, feel free to add them in, as in:

```
"getting started" showing GSD
```

for a world of tips about showing your German shepard. (GSD is German Shepard Dog—all of those in-the-know use the acronym.)

Or, suppose you're really into aviation. Check into a Usenet search for:

```
newsgroups:aviation.homebuilt getting started
```

for tons of information on—what else—getting started with building your own aircraft and related paraphernalia.

government

If you're interested in getting all you can out of your tax money, be sure to take advantage of the government information available free on the Internet. Just a quick search for:

```
government
```

produces a number of links to information. If you need specific information and, for whatever reason, particularly want governmental sources, you can always try a domain search of the Web. For example, to find information about taxes (ugh!) from only government sources, you'd search for:

```
domain:gov taxes
```

On the other hand, if you want to see some of the cool things that the Library of Congress is doing, just search for:

```
host:loc.gov exhibit
```

We assure you, it's almost as good as a museum. Speaking of which, a search for:

```
Smithsonian Institution
```

gives you a whole list of the online presentations that the Smithsonian makes available.

H

hand-held computers

If computers are so much fun that you have to take one everywhere and you think that the newest notebook computers are far too big and clunky to use effectively, try:

```
hand-held computers
```

Really! This search gives you loads of information on this technology. Or, if you're looking for specific models, try something like:

```
hand-held computers +newton
```

Over on the Usenet side, you'll probably want to get some input from other users before you take the plunge into hand-held computing.

In Search of Health

In a comment about AltaVista Search, Kala wrote:

I teach health policy to graduate students. I currently have a class of nine with mostly clinical backgrounds, several with little or no computing experience. I put them online and showed them how to access AltaVista (you are at the top of a page I have organized for them to use in doing health policy research.) Within ten minutes each had completed and refined a search for their paper topic. The ease and intuitiveness of the system was clearly motivating even the ones with no prior experience (and anyone with none today has had some phobia about working online). They were all excited and enthusiastic and sold on the capacity to do research online. Thank you for a terrific teaching tool.

Kala Ladenheim

---

herbs

Herbs? No, not your Uncle Herb (although you could check out "acquaintances" or "genealogy" in this chapter). You can look up *herbs*, those tasty weed-looking things you add to your food. For general information, enter:

```
herbs
```

which gives you general information about different kinds of herbs as well as cooking with them and growing them. If you want to narrow your search, you can enter:

```
herbs growing
herbs recipes
```

or:

```
herb* medicine
```

These searches provide you with information on herbs as they pertain to the specific use you're looking for. If you're interested in the latest discussions and opinions, try a Usenet search for:

```
herb* medicine
```

Also, take a look at the search ideas in the "cooking" section of this chapter.

hexadecimal

What the hex is that?

Don't you get tired of seeing "hexadecimal" thrown around like it made sense? Just check with the Web and you'll get the real meaning. A search like:

```
"hexadecimal number" "what is"
```

brings up several pages with definitions or explanations.

hiccups

Have you ever wondered what causes hiccups? Now you can find out! If you do a Simple Search for:

```
hiccups
```

you'll find all sorts of information on the causes and some recommended cures for those racking hiccups. You can even find specific information on, for example, those tiny hiccups an unborn baby makes by narrowing your search, like this:

```
+hiccups +prenatal
```

home repair—electrical

Just can't figure out what to do about that persistent problem with fuses blowing?
Try a Simple Search for:

```
fuse blow*
```

If you're concerned about the fuses and your household wiring in particular, you
could always add:

```
fuse blow* +house wiring
```

or:

```
"house wiring" +"circuit breaker"
```

If everything works, but you just can't figure out why the light switch gets so
hot, check into:

```
"fire code"
```

or:

```
"fire code" +electrical
```

home repair—plumbing

On the other hand, maybe you're tired of paying the big bucks for a plumber to come
and take care of what looks like an easy repair. (It never fails that the plumbing backs
up on a Sunday afternoon when you have six relatives visiting, right?) Do it yourself!
Just search for:

```
plumbing instructions
```

One tip: before you start, do a quick search for:

```
plumbing contractor
```

or:

```
"repair* water damage"
```

in case something goes wrong.

In Search of Homework

In a comment about AltaVista Search, Cathy wrote:

I had to write to say that this site is a terrific Internet tool. Tonight my son (who lives in Brookings, OR) called me to say his jr. high math teacher had asked them to find out what "sociable numbers" are. None of my limited reference books had the term & in Sacramento we have very limited library services. So I looked it up here, and we were able to discover what the term means and what a aliquot cycle is. I would have never found it without you. And having found it, I was able to bring current research from the University of Connecticut. to a youngster living at the edge of nowhere. Thanks a million!

Cathy Horiuchi

---

horse

I wish I may, I wish I might, I wish to have a pony. Heck, I'd take a horse, too. If you need some information before diving into equine ownership, try searching for:

```
horse
```

on the Web to find everything from horse museums to information about specific breeds and horse care. Alternatively:

```
equine
```

produces more scientific or medical links, such as equine reproduction or equine clinics. Usenet searches for:

```
horse
```

or:

```
equine
```

produce thousands of links, mostly about horse health. If you just want to see horse discussions, try a search for:

```
newsgroups:equestrian
```

You might find other search ideas under "zoo" in this chapter. Check it out!

hovercraft

Sure enough, even "hovercraft" have made it to the Web. Just a search for:

```
hovercraft
```

gives you links to pictures, schedules, and hovercraft for sale.

humor

A great way to find the funny of the day is to search in Usenet. For the more or less complete rundown on the latest (usually heavily recycled) humor, search for:

```
newsgroups:rec.humor -newsgroups:rec.humor*.d
```

to get all the jokes (but not the discussion in the .d groups) from the humor group. You can also search for:

```
humor -tasteless
```

if you want to avoid the—er, um—tasteless jokes out there. (Actually, it excludes only the messages clearly labeled as such, but it's a start.) Unfortunately, there's no way to find only the truly hilarious jokes, but:

```
newsgroups:rec.humor.funny
```

usually has some good material. See for yourself!

Also, on the Web side of things, thousands of sites claim humor. Try searching for specific kinds such as:

```
humor limericks
```

(

In Search of Ice Cores
In response to a discussion of religion and the age of the earth, Kevin wrote:

There have been projects in Greenland and the Antarctic where the layers are particularly thick.

But as for specifics, you might go to altavista.digital.com and search for +Greenland +"ice core". You'll get about 400 hits. Near the top of the list is "GRIP Greenland Ice Core Data, Paleoclimate Data; NGDC (EARTH_LAND_NGDC_PALEO_GRIP1" which says that a particular ice core taken in 1991 goes back 250,000 years. I guess if there were a big layer of dirt from the Flood of Noah, they would have mentioned it ;-)

If you add +Noah to your search string, then you will skip the pure science and get into the polemics.

Kevin Davidson (kwdavids@mercury.interpath.com)

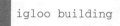

igloo

You'll probably have to print the information and take it with you, but be prepared with instructions for winter wilderness survival. Try a Simple Web Search on:

```
igloo building
```

to find out how you can build an igloo of your own. Or to seek out a broader perspective on the topic, try:

```
"native american" living indian* igloo eskimo
```

This search provides links to information on why and how igloos became a part of Inuit living. If, on the other hand, you're more interested in the wilderness aspect than the Inuit angle, try a Usenet search for:

```
newsgroups:backcountry survival
```

indoor plants

Are your houseplants dying faster than you can buy new ones? Wondering how to get that green thumb you've always wanted? Do a quick Web search for:

```
houseplants
```

This search provides you with tons of information about indoor plants, including tips on plant care, information on which types will grow best in your household, and ideas on purchasing plants. You can even find out why your favorite plant seems to be withering away. Just do a Usenet search for:

```
+plants dead dying
```

If you know enough about the plant to be more specific, by all means do so. For example, a Usenet search for:

```
jade plant dropping leaves
```

works wonders, if you have a jade plant that's, well, dropping leaves. If you just have to have plants but all means of keeping them alive fail, try a different type:

```
+cactus +plant newsgroups:garden
```

Cultivate your knowledge about cactus plants (we hear they're practically impossible to kill!).

See also "gardening" in this chapter for more ideas on plant-related searches.

investments

Thinking about investing? Not sure you're ready to call a broker? Try doing some research on the Internet. A Usenet search can provide you with advice and answers to questions. Just enter:

```
+investment advice +newsgroups:invest*
```

If you don't want to hear the online sales pitches, you can try:

```
+investment advice +newsgroups:invest* -guaran*
```

which weeds out the "guaranteed" investments. You can also check out the Web for investment information by typing:

```
+investment advice
```

This search yields a number of scholarly articles and apparently sound information.

J

jargon

The world of computers is filled with jargon, most of it remarkably arcane and hard to decipher, including *SCSI, hacker* or *cracker, kluge,* and *abend,* to name only a few. To find the meaning of these and practically any other jargon terms, search the Web for:

```
jargon dictionary
```

Not only can you go out and buy a dictionary of jargon, you can also search out the meanings right on the Web with a couple of quick clicks. That is, if someone calls you a "suit" in an apparently derogatory way, do a search for:

```
+jargon +suit
```

jazz

Now here's something to get jazzed about! All that jazz, ready to be seen, heard, and enjoyed, awaits at:

```
+jazz festival
```

With this search, you'll find all sorts of links to information about jazz festivals, their histories, and their growing popularity. If you'd rather experience intimate improv sessions, or even get into making the music yourself, try:

```
+jazz improv*
```

If you can't play the music without an instrument, get one through a Web search for:

```
music instrument +"for sale"
```

Over on the Usenet side, you'd be well-advised to include the name of the instrument (unless you're pretty multitalented), like this:

```
+"for sale" saxophone
```

should get you anything you need, except perhaps a booking on Leno:

```
+"tonight show" +"Jay Leno"
```

jobs

The Internet is *the* place to look for job postings. If you're just browsing (and want to browse through a lot!), try a Simple Usenet Search for:

```
newsgroups:jobs
```

This search results in lots of listings, probably more than you can wade through, so you might focus your search slightly, for example, like this:

```
newsgroups:misc.jobs
```

The misc.jobs newsgroup is where many postings are found. If you have a local set of newsgroups, such as ba. for the Bay Area, or ok. for Oklahoma, you might head for Advanced Search so you can add that:

```
newsgroups:(ok.jobs or ba.jobs)
```

Of course, if you're looking for a specific sort of job, you could add that in the ranking area of the Advanced Search, but you shouldn't be too specific:

```
newsgroups:(ok.jobs or ba.jobs)
```

If you're a writer, you'd put:

```
writer
```

in the ranking field. And there you go! All the jobs you'd ever want.

Using AltaVista to search the Web can also help you find specific jobs at specific companies. Suppose you're interested in a job as a marketing assistant at a local company called Symmetrix, a management consulting firm in Lexington, Massachusetts. First, try searching for:

```
Symmetrix
```

which gives you hundreds of hits, many of which deal with computer systems with that name. Since you're looking for a specific company by that name, try:

```
Symmetrix "management consulting"
```

and you get the site of the company you want.

If you knew your potential employer's name, you could search for it on the Web and in newsgroups to find out his or her background and interests. Doing so before the big interview could give you an edge over other applicants.

K

keys/locks

Just because you locked your keys in the car doesn't mean that you're out of luck. AltaVista Search to the rescue! Just search for:

```
lock key
```

or for:

```
locksmith
```

These searches provide you with links to locksmiths who have Web sites. You'll probably save some time if you also add your location, like this:

```
lock key +Berkeley
```

Heck, if you hurry, you'll be able to get the doors unlocked so you can get in and put the top up! By the way, if you make a habit of this (or if you have kids who play with the bathroom locks), you might search for:

```
lockpick* kids
```

In Search of a Kid's Story

In a comment about AltaVista Search, Don wrote:

I was showing one of our recalcitrant users just how broad Web info is when we decided to search for something truly unusual and quintessentially Australian. We fed in "Mulga Bill's bicycle," the name of a reasonably well-known kid's story from many years ago. We got 15 hits in the blink of an eye. Most impressive.

Don Ewart

kites

Oh, go fly a kite! What? You don't have one, and you say the tree down the street always takes the kite for lunch anyway? Turn to the experts in a Usenet search for:

```
kites
```

If you have specific issues to discuss, such as lights for kites (really!), try:

```
newsgroups:kites lights
```

If the weather's bad, just search over on the Web for:

```
+indoor +kite instructions building
```

knitting

When you've just got to find something to occupy your hands while you're waiting for those Web pages to download, do what German university students do in class to pass the time—knit! For starters, try entering:

`knitting`

This would give you information not only about newsletters and shows, but also about discussion forums where you can share tips and ideas.

Check out other knitting search ideas under "blind" in this chapter. Cool stuff!

L

lace-making

Although you might have thought that lace came only on big spools in the fabric store, you'll be pleased to learn that you can make your own, and the Web can tell you how. Just use AltaVista and search for:

`lacemaking`

This Simple Search finds a surprisingly long list of resources, ranging from materials to actual how-tos. Searching for:

`lace`

gets into a whole different world—something about "leather and . . ."

language

Just can't go on without brushing up on your language knowledge? Try:

`language learning`

or:

```
language acquisition
```

to get the latest information about how people learn languages. Throwing in old Noam, as in:

```
language acquisition +Chomsky
```

gives you the whole black box theory, online. To narrow it down a little more, try:

```
+language acquisition +children
```

and see how your kids (or you, as a kid) did it. Also see "foreign language and culture" in this chapter for more neat language search ideas.

lesson plans

If you're a teacher and completely out of ideas for that lesson coming up, try searching the Web for:

```
"lesson plan*"
```

You'll find hundreds of prepackaged lesson plans, ready for use. Many of these have been successfully used by teachers around the world! Add the subject or area for a more precise result, as in:

```
"lesson plan*" +german
"lesson plan*" +science
```

or:

```
"lesson plan*" +health
```

Ahhh! To be in fifth grade again and make an aquarium. . . . Those were the days.

In Search of Librarians

In a comment about AltaVista Search, Allison wrote:

I am so glad I happened on your site. Your search engine is by far the slickest I have used. As a librarian, I appreciate the scope of information to which you provide access. I found a picture of Diana Ross, the dimensions of the Statue of Liberty, and the names and addresses of shops selling brass compasses all in one short session. I am telling others about your service. Thanks again.

Allison Williams

---

lighthouses

Lighthouses, too, find a home on the Web. A search for:

```
lighthouse picture
```

produces links to pictures of lighthouses around the world. If you're more into the magic and romance than just seeing a picture, try:

```
lighthouse cookbook
```

to eat as the lighthouse keepers did, or:

```
lighthouse book
```

to read the stories of how lighthouses were built as well as how they were used and maintained. If you're interested in buying a lighthouse, a search like:

AltaVista Search · OnSite Knowledge · Advanced · Simple · Private eXtension Products · Help

```
+lighthouse sell buy sale real estate
```

should produce any leads available on the Web.

In Search of Logan's Run

In reference to a question about the movie *Logan's Run,* Cassie wrote:

I did a Simple Search in AltaVista and found the FAQ here (first try!)

http://www2.zoom.com/personal/tracer/LogansRun

If you ever want to try AltaVista (great search engine), the URL is:

http://altavista.digital.com/

Cassie Chamberlain

---

lyrics

AltaVista Search can open the door to the lyrics of thousands of songs. Try a search for the title of your favorite, or just head for lyrics archives to choose from thousands. A search for:

```
"Louie Louie"
```

yields hundreds of "definitive" versions of the lyrics to this frat party standard.

Take a look at "music" in this chapter for more information about searching for song titles and albums.

M

marketing research

Suppose you are a supplier of Internet products and services. You do business mainly through distributors, so there are many customers using your products that you have never dealt with directly. Many of those may choose to display your company's logo at their site. Those that do will probably keep the original filename for the .GIF file of your logo. If you work for Digital Equipment, you might search:

```
+image:digital.gif -url:digital.com
```

because you are only interested in finding non-Digital sites. You get about 5000 hits, many of which in fact do display Digital's logo. (Others simply have given the name DIGITAL.GIF to other graphics files.) The name *AltaVista* is more distinctive and rare, and a search for:

```
+image:altavist*.gif -url:digital.com
```

yields about 800 matches. (You search for *altavist** rather than just *altavista* because many systems are limited to names of eight characters.) In this case, it looks like nearly all the matches are good ones.

You might be tempted to use the same technique to do research on banner advertising on the Web. At first it would seem that a search for the filename of the GIF used for a banner would match all sites now running that ad. But many (probably most) Web sites with paid advertising rotate which banner appears. So it would be random luck whether the GIF you are looking for happened to be displayed when AltaVista Search visited to index the page.

In Search of Mars

In reference to a question linking Carl Sagan to faces found on Mars, Dave wrote:

I think Carl Sagan would rather jump through a burning ring of fire than have his name associated with the Mars Face other than in a debunking manner.

　However, check these out:

http://www.fau.edu/barton/mars.html [plus links]
http://www.seds.org/nodes/NODEv5n7-2.html
http://altavista.digital.com/cgi-bin/query?pg=q&what=web&fmt=
　　.&q=%2Bmars%2Bface

　That last URL is for an AltaVista search result which will give you a bazillion pro/con/whatever references on the subject. Certainly, more references than I could list here.
　By the way, I highly recommend AltaVista [http://altavista. digital.com] for any serious Web or Usenet searches. There are a lot of search engines out there, for a lot of different purposes, but for the Web and the Usenet you're not going to find an engine with the depth and up-to-date qualities of AltaVista. If you read the search instructions carefully so that you know how to get around, you'll be amazed at the results it gives.

Dave Locke

---

medical topics—general

AltaVista Search lets you find a vast range of information on medical topics. Of course, AltaVista Search *cannot* take the place of a visit or phone call to your doctor, but it can provide you with a good place to start researching.

AltaVista Search is a great way to glean medical information and anecdotal data. Start by searching for specific conditions, the more specific the better. For example, suppose you've been experiencing lower back pain, you can enter the Simple Search:

```
"lower back pain"
```

This search gives you a wide variety of information on the causes and remedies for common lower back problems. If you've noticed other symptoms that accompany the back pain, you can enter those as well:

```
"lower back pain" "leg"
```

This more specific search narrows the results to just those that apply to the symptoms you entered.

Or suppose you just came home from the doctor with a prescription and want to know what kinds of side effects to expect. Instead of dragging out that huge *Physicians Desk Reference* (PDR), just look it up using AltaVista Search. For example, for information on a specific drug, just enter the name, like this:

```
"Tylenol 3"
```

medical topics—rare

Normally, the rarer a medical condition, the more difficult it is to find information about it or to get in touch with others who have experienced it. With AltaVista Search, rarity is an advantage, helping you to get to what you want quickly. For instance, a Simple Search of the Web for:

```
"Opitz Syndrome"
```

yields a list of a couple of dozen pages, all of which are on target, including explanations of the condition as well as parent support groups. Likewise, a Simple Search of the Web for:

```
"sensory integrative dysfunction"
```

provides a couple of dozen useful matches.

medical topics—specific

Your child, born with cleft lip/cleft palate, is now a teenager and is scheduled for cosmetic nose surgery (rhinoplasty). You'd like to learn whatever you can about this procedure—especially in cases involving cleft lip. First you try a Simple Search of the Web:

```
+"cleft lip" +rhinoplasty
```

That yields dozens of matches, many of which are lists of the capabilities of medical institutions that do reconstructive plastic surgery. You'd prefer information that specifically links the condition of cleft lip with the procedure of rhinoplasty. So try Advanced Search and use the NEAR command, like this:

```
"cleft lip" NEAR rhinoplasty
```

That yields useful information on rhinoplasty, but still with no connection to cleft lip. So you'd like to check for parent support groups, some of whose members' children might have gone through a similar operation.

```
+"cleft lip" +parent* support
```

That helps you locate Prescription Parents and other such organizations.

In Search of Medical Information

In a note about AltaVista Search, Jim and Alison wrote:

I just thought I'd send a note of appreciation to you as I've just used your page to search for information on chicken pox, which my five-year-old son has contracted. The amount of info forwarded by your page was amazing, and has turned us into the "world's most knowledgeable" on the subject!

Jim & Alison Hanner

---

meetings

You've just been nominated to plan your company's annual board meeting that will take place in San Diego. Gads! You need to find a hotel, meeting rooms, transportation—the whole shebang. You can start by searching the Web, like this:

```
+hotel + "San Diego"
```

You get about 200 matches, many of which look like they are right on target. From there, you can narrow the search to a specific hotel and search for meeting rooms and prices, as in:

```
+"San Diego" +Ramada "meeting rooms"
```

Many organizations, such as car rental companies, provide prices—or at least contact information—on their Web sites. So, if you're looking for prices on car rental, just enter the *company name* plus *price,* like this:

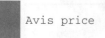

```
Avis price
```

metal

As part of your job, you have to be on the lookout for suppliers of sheet metal for backplanes, preferably ones located in Massachusetts. Try Advanced Search of the Web, like this:

```
("sheet metal" AND backplane) AND (Massachusetts OR Mass OR MA)
```

Or suppose you inherited gold coins and want to know their current value. Try entering the search:

```
"precious metal" +gold
```

This search gives you records of the price of gold and links to other information about gold.

In Search of Magic

In response to a question about a magic-oriented Web page, possibly created by Michael Patterson, Jeff wrote:

I found it in a couple of minutes using AltaVista:

   (http://altavista.digital.com/), query "Michael Patterson"+magic.

Everybody ought to bookmark AltaVista. Try it!

Jeffery Boes (boes@zds.com)

money

To see if money is just waiting for you to pick up, do a Simple Search for:

```
"unclaimed refunds"
```

No kidding! An increasing number of states and institutions post on the Web lists of tax and other refunds that individuals have not yet collected. Maybe there's an unclaimed refund with your name on it.

Also, try an Advanced Search for:

```
(unclaimed AND bequest*) OR (missing AND heir*)
```

That yields about 3000 matches, many of which are references to TV shows with those elements in the plot. So refine the search, like this:

```
(unclaimed AND bequest*) OR (missing AND heir*) AND NOT (TV
OR television)
```

That narrows the field to 2000. But if you seriously think that there might be money coming to you, it might be well worth your while to enter other relevant words or even check them all.

movies

Just have to have more information about a specific movie? Can't remember who played which role? Just search for the movie by name in a Web Simple Search, as in:

```
Braveheart
```

Need to find a good—no, great—flick for weekend viewing? Review pages about the winners to help you decide:

```
oscar winner "best picture"
```

On the other hand, if you're just looking for a quick film clip to play on your computer to verify that the computer really is the powerful beast the salesman assured you it was, search for:

```
movie archives download +trailer
```

In Search of Movies

In reference to a movie allegedly based on the old role-playing game Zork, Kathleen wrote:

I did an AltaVista search for zork movie and found a page that said Activation and Threshold Media had agreed to make a movie and TV series based on the Zork game.

Kathleen S. MacPherson

music

AltaVista Search plays to the tune of thousands of music topics. Check these out, just for a demo. Suppose you'd like to have some lyrics of French songs. All you have to do is search the Web by entering *song,* like this:

```
song
```

This search gives you thousands of hits—er, um—song titles, as well as information on songs and music in general and even a country song naming contest. You might try narrowing the search by entering words from the song title or the album title, like this:

```
"I'm just a bill"
```

or:

```
"schoolhouse rock"
```

These searches give you, among other things, a link to the Schoolhouse Rock series of kids' music. (You remember these, don't you? . . . "I'm just a bill, yes I'm only a bill, and I'm sittin' here on Capitol Hill. . . .)

AltaVista Search can even help you book your band for gigs. Try searching newsgroups for:

```
+guitar +gig* +wanted
```

With this search, you can find all sorts of organizations advertising for entertainment help. Just what you're looking for!

Along those same lines, suppose you are interested in a band, but aren't sure how the name is spelled. You think that it's "Verucha Salt" or "Berucha Salt" but aren't sure. Searches on those phrases yield nothing. So you search for the name of one of their songs, "Seether," on the Web, which immediately gives you a long list of pages devoted to "Veruca Salt." Now, knowing the right spelling, you search for the group's name and get over 1000 good matches. Following those links, you might be tempted to buy a CD at one of the commercial Web sites. For instance, "American Thighs" sells for about $16 (including shipping). But before placing your order, you should search for the same CD in the newsgroups:

```
+"Veruca Salt" +"for sale" +"American Thighs"
```

where dozens of individuals are offering it for sale (in "mint" condition) for $7 or $8.

In Search of Music

In reference to a question about an October Project CD, Chad wrote:

They are more of a college alternative band, actually (although some of the elements of this band might appeal to Enya/Lorenna McKennit fans)... I believe they are just five people from a particular college (forget which one) that formed a band and got discovered. There are about four or five Web pages on them, which searching AltaVista (http://altavista.digital.com/) for october+project will find.

Chad Gould

N

name that publication (or web site)

With the vast numbers of Web sites and online publications, it is becoming increasingly difficult to think up a unique name for a new one. AltaVista Search helps you quickly test your ideas, to see if someone else is already using that same name. For example, try a Simple Search of the Web for:

```
"Internet to go"
```

There are too many matches to try them all. But a quick check determines that many are just random appearances of those three words in order, such as "...Internet. To go...." Try *Internet to Go,* capitalizing "Go" as would be more likely in the name of a publication or Web site. As it turns out, a company named Solution Point recently announced a product with that name. If what you plan to do does not in any way compete with that product and couldn't be confused with it, you might consider using a typographical variant, such as Internet2Go, which yields (as of now) zero matches.

names

If the stork's arrival is just any day now but you don't have a good name picked out, do a Simple Search for:

```
selecting choosing "baby name*"
```

Everything from lists to programs that provide choices for baby names will appear. On the other hand, if your interest in names is ... different, search for:

```
"hurricane names"
```

If you want, you can ensure that your child's name will be the first hurricane of the 1999 hurricane season in the Atlantic Ocean (that is, Arlene).

NASCAR races

Just can't get to the TV for the latest on the NASCAR races? Do a Web search for:

```
NASCAR
```

(yes, use all caps) and keep up with the results and follow along with driver profiles.

natural history

If you're losing sleep because you just don't know how old the earth is, check with AltaVista Search. A Simple Search for:

```
earth age
```

should get you going with geological, biblical, and other interpretations of the age of the earth.

New Age

Suppose you're researching New Age religions or even thinking about joining one. AltaVista Search can provide you with scads of information. For example, check out a Usenet search, like this:

```
newsgroups:newage
```

This search brings up a variety of discussions and opinions about religion, generally in the context of New Age religion. You can also check out New Age music by searching Usenet using the phrase:

```
"new age music"
```

for discussions on this topic. Or try the same search on the Web to find everything from samples to description to reviews.

news archives

Even though the Web doesn't land in your bushes each morning, it's still a good source of news. Try a Web search for:

```
newsstand headlines today
```

You'll find links to a number of sites that provide news online. Although many of the sites provide only some information for free and require a subscription for the whole story, it's a quick and easy way to catch up on the headlines.

O

opinions

Just the facts, ma'am, just the facts. Or actually, you can even find opinions, ma'am. Do a Usenet search, any Usenet search, and you'll get more opinions than you probably bargained for. Sometimes these differences of opinion result in "flame wars," in which heated opinions and insults are exchanged.

If you just want an interactive editorial page, try searching for the controversial topic of your choice, along with *newsgroups:talk.* For example, enter:

```
taxes newsgroups:talk
```

or:

```
newsgroups:alt.politics "government size"
```

Keep in mind, though, that these (and similar editorial pages) are just like the opinion page of your newspaper—you might not agree with the opinion.

In Search of Old Friends

Deb wrote:

I have a friend that I've kept in touch with for over twenty years—since we were in first grade together. Unfortunately, after I got married and moved a few times, we lost touch. I tried an AltaVista search for his first and last name; then I tried his first and last name plus the state in which he had last lived. I finally tried his first and last name, plus his profession, like this

> *"firstname lastname" +music*

Interestingly, I found him through a music company's Web site that listed his latest CD. Outstanding!

Deb Rowe

---

outdoor activities

Suppose you've had enough of the computer and Internet world and need to get away—really away. (It *could* happen, you know.) Before you hit the power switch and wander off into the great outdoors, try out a Usenet search on outdoor-related topics, for example:

```
newsgroups:backcountry survival skills
```

You'll find useful information on surviving your adventure as well as tips to make the most of it. You can even find great debates to ponder, such as a discussion of cotton versus polyester sports gear.

Over on the Web, you find more substance and less talk with a search for:

```
"survival skills" outdoor
```

After you've decided to tame your trip and not camp out with the bears, you might try a Simple Search for:

```
outdoor recreation camping backpacking
```

Have a good trip!

P

parenting

From traditional parenting to caring for elderly parents, a Web search for:

```
parenting
```

produces thousands of hits. With this search, you find links to the latest tips and trends as well as tried-and-true techniques. If you're looking for specific information, try narrowing your search, like this:

```
parenting infants
```

This Simple Search brings up resources specifically geared toward the wee ones, while:

```
"child development" theory
```

provides sites that explain exactly what is going on every step of the way. You can also check out Usenet discussions, which provide perspectives that theory and textbooks rarely offer about raising children. You can find discussions on topics from:

```
child development
```

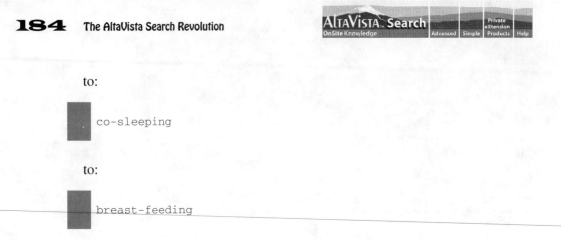

to:

```
co-sleeping
```

to:

```
breast-feeding
```

These Usenet discussions open new sets of opinions and incredible varieties of information, from strictly scientific to views from all camps of child-rearing.

peanut butter

Just can't stand the thought of another peanut butter and jelly sandwich? You've heard of peanut butter and orange juice but it sounds pretty bad to you? Just search for:

```
peanut butter
```

and collect all kinds of recipes, including several enticing variants on chocolate peanut butter. If you're a peanut butter fan and tend to overdo, search for:

```
"peanut butter" +choking
```

Also check out "cooking" as well as the user story on "recipes" in this chapter for even more search ideas.

personality profile

If you're interested in personality profiles (those silly tests that know more about the inner workings of your psyche than you'll ever admit, even to your spouse), do a Usenet or Web search for:

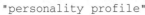

```
"personality profile"
```

Or, you can choose a specific personality test, like:

```
myers-briggs
```

You can even take a Myers-Briggs test right on your very own computer. Try searching for:

```
myers-briggs taking
```

photography

Suppose you just got a great camera and want to know more about taking pictures. A general search for:

```
photograph*
```

yields all kinds of stuff—focusing, so to speak, would help. For example, if you want how-to information, try:

```
photograph* techniques
```

You can even find information on specific photographers, like:

```
photograph* "Ansel Adams"
```

As always, rare words help. For example, try:

```
daguerreotype
```

for links to information on old photographs, online reproductions, or even an article by Edgar Allan Poe about daguerreotypes. Or if you're looking for photos on a particular topic, enter:

to get the use policies and some space photos. Or try:

```
pictur* +NASA
```

to go directly to space pictures. Really!

   You can even keep up with the latest art photography trends by searching for:

```
lomography
```

poetry

"Whose woods these are I think I know...." If you don't know and want to find out more about this Robert Frost poem, let AltaVista Search help you out. Start with a Web search for:

```
"Robert Frost" woods
```

to find out more on this poem. Or try:

```
newsgroups:arts.poem*
```

to find in-depth and involved poetry analysis on a range of poets and poetry. If you're not much into analysis, just search for:

```
poetry newsgroups:marketplace
```

to seek out used poetry books for sale.

publishing

Just about through with the Great American Novel? Need to find a publisher? Simple. Search for:

```
publisher contact information book fiction
```

or search by the publisher's name. If you get tired of sending your manuscripts to ungrateful publishers without the common sense to select your novel out of the hundreds they get each week, just look into:

```
self-publishing
```

and do it yourself.

Or suppose you are a publisher of children's books and believe that there is a market for fiction that deals with divorce and that involves pets. You'd also like to check what the competition has in print already, but since most online book catalogs are in databases, AltaVista Search would not have that information in its index. But you'd also like to check the marketplace, looking for all references to such books on the Web. And, ideally, you'd like to find works of that kind that are available on the Web that have not yet been published in print. You try a Simple Search of the Web:

```
+fiction + child* +divorce*
```

That gives you 1000 matches. Refining the search to look for unpublished works:

```
+fiction +child* +divorce* +unpublished
```

gives you about sixty to check out.

politics

Yes, politics have even invaded the Internet. For the most timely information, do a Usenet search for:

```
"us politics"
```

This search provides you with all sorts of vehement opinions about every aspect of U.S. politics. You can also search for:

```
government conspiracy
```

which yields the world of entertaining reading you'd expect from a search on the word *paranoia*. Searching for your favorite political party on the Web would be fruitful. Just enter:

```
Republican
Democrat
```

or even the name of your favorite candidate, like this:

```
"candidate name goes within quotes"
```

However, you'll find more interesting information and heated discussion by searching for specific topics, such as:

```
federal tax*
reaganomics
```

or:

```
immigration
```

Q

quilting

If you or someone you know enjoys quilting, a quick AltaVista search for *quilt** works wonders. If you have something in particular in mind, you could always try:

```
quilt* +"Double Wedding Ring" +pattern
+quilting +lessons
```

Alternatively, you could branch out into:

```
+needle +crafts
+Arts +Crafts
```

In Search of Quilts

In reference to a discussion about quilt pattern ideas, Susan wrote:

There are a lot of X-files Web sites out there with great graphics for ideas—do a search with AltaVista or one of the other good search engines and do some surfing for quilt ideas. Sounds like fun.

Susan Drudings

quotations

AltaVista Search is a great resource for checking out quotations, from the mundane to the cliché. The old gag about "I'd rather have a bottle in front of me than a frontal lobotomy"—well, it's actually the title of an old country and western song. Type:

```
"rather have a bottle in front"
```

It's also good for identifying the clever sayings that you probably don't want on your Web page because everyone else has already done it. For an enormous collection of diverse Web sites, try:

```
"knowledge is power"
```

In search of Quotations

For several weeks, a co-worker has had on the dry-erase board beside his desk the incomplete quotation "_____ is the last refuge of the incompetent." It had become a game for others at the office to guess the missing word and author. No one really knew.

I submitted the query in various forms to more than one search engine and found some interesting data, but not the authentic quote. From AltaVista I not only matched multiple good sites, but found a complete reference to Isaac Asimov's essays (the author). The missing word is "Violence."

Morris Shaw

R

radio

You can talk to people around the world and don't even need a telephone! A ham radio is just the trick. For starters, try a Web search for:

```
"ham radio" sale
```

and:

```
+"ham radio" +regulations
```

for information about purchasing and using a ham radio. Also, you can find information about ham radios in general and the people who use them just by entering:

```
ham radio
```

In Search of Research

In a comment about AltaVista Search, Ian wrote:

I was doing research for a science fiction novel. I remembered from college, talk about a drug/medication/drink that caused your vision to change so that you seemed to be wearing yellow tinted glasses. This was an important fact in the novel. I typed in a command to AltaVista, something like +"distorted vision" +yellow +drug and within two seconds found a tea of sorts that is made from a plant that only grows in Mexico—the tea gives you a mild high like beer but if you take too much, you end up with yellow vision the following day—this worked perfectly into the outline for the novel and caused me to wonder what other source of information on the planet could have found that information in two seconds—what does this mean to man—what does it mean to potentially have every written word indexed in one place where it can be found in two seconds—it means tremendous progress for man, and it also means that there is potentially the DEFINITIVE site—if it is not there—it doesn't exist.

Ian Ferguson

real estate

Planning to relocate? Let AltaVista Search help! Although it can't pack your boxes or lift your grand piano, it can find relocation assistance Web sites as well as cost-of-living calculators. For starters, try searching the Web for:

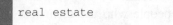

```
real estate
```

This search even finds real estate listings around the world! If you're just looking for a real estate agent, search for *real estate* and the *location,* as in:

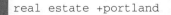

```
real estate +portland
```

Also, you can find information about the place you want to move by entering *quality of life* plus the city, like this:

```
"quality of life" +portland
```

In Search of Recipes

In the context of a discussion of great Russian black bread, Kathleen wrote:

An AltaVista Search using the keywords "Russian Black Bread" yields many recipes. The first two are:

> *http://www.ts.umu.se/~effie/rec.food.recipes/breads/yeast/black*
> *http://www3.epicurious.com/HyperNews/get/archive_*
> *swap1101-1200/1187.html*

Kathleen Seidel

roller coaster

Does your very existence turn on the trips to the state fair or nearest amusement park so you can ride the roller coaster? Or, maybe you'd prefer to read up on the roller coaster rather than actually having to hold on to your stomach for the whole trip? Try a Web search for:

```
roller coaster
```

or, if you're a traditionalist:

```
wooden roller coaster
```

to find out where to get to the old time coasters. If you're more on the cautious side, there's always:

```
roller coaster safety
```

To discuss the physics of roller coasters, head to a Usenet search for:

```
newsgroups:roller-coaster physics
```

In Search of Research

In a comment about AltaVista Search, Marty wrote:

I just thought I would let you know how much I appreciate AltaVista. I am working on my doctorate and your search tool is a lifesaver!!!! How fortunate we are to have your services in the Internet. I will forever be grateful to all of you. Believe me I will always tell everyone that AltaVista was instrumental in helping me complete my degree. Here is a big thanks!

Marty Spitzer

S

scanner

So, you say you just bought a new scanner and want to scan every picture from your albums? No problem! Just try a Simple Search on the Web for:

```
+scanning tips FAQ
```

This search gives you all sorts of tips and tricks to making the most of your scanner and the scanned results. After you have that down (or possibly before), you'll need to do a search on:

```
"graphic* format" minimizing size
```

to learn about the different formats available and how to maintain quality without running completely out of disk space. Next, of course, you'll need information on:

```
disk compression
```

to try to squeeze as much space as you can out of the drive. Finally, the next step is to do a Web search for:

```
+title:"hard drive" +advice
```

to get information on more efficiently using your disk as well as on eventually purchasing a new drive. Of course, a Usenet search on:

```
buying "hard drive"
```

is also a useful place to start. See where buying that new scanner got you?

shareware

Shareware (try-it-before-you-buy-it software) is readily available on the Internet. To find it, just search in the Web for the word shareware and your computer operating system, like this:

```
shareware Windows95
shareware Macintosh
shareware OS/2
```

or:

```
shareware unix
```

You'll have your choice of dozens of shareware libraries. Do be sure to read the licensing agreements—the software isn't free, just free to evaluate. If you keep using it beyond a certain point, you must pay for it.

In Search of Side Effects

Emily wrote:

"My doctor prescribed a new drug for me, and the product literature didn't tell me about what the potential side effects might be in language I could relate to. I used AltaVista to search the newsgroups for "side effects" and the drug's name and found not only exactly what I was after but also the names of several newsgroups that discussed a wealth of prescription drug information."

Emily Julien

skating

If you're tired of sitting at the computer, get your gear and head out to go skating. Do a Simple Search (Web or Usenet) for:

```
skating rink
```

if you're not sure where to go. If you need some help, try a Web search for:

```
"learning to skate"
```

for tips you can give your little one (or yourself!). You might also need:

```
"skating equipment" buy* sale rent
```

or even:

```
+"first aid" +skating +injury
```

Read up on Colles' fracture!

software

If you run your own company, say, an Internet Service Provider (ISP), you may well want to locate billing software tailored for your needs. A Simple Search of the Web for:

```
+"billing software" +ISP
```

leads to a wide variety of packages you can choose from.

souvenir

Just have to get the t-shirt, even if you haven't been there or done that? Not only will

```
souvenir
```

find all kinds of sites about souvenirs, with the site and a good credit card, you can buy them too. If you'd ever longed for an authentic Manx cat t-shirt, direct from the Isle of Man, you're set now! Search for:

```
souvenir Isle of Man
```

If you don't care much about the souvenir as long as you get to take a virtual tour, there's always the Magic Kingdom, accessible through a Simple Web search for:

```
Disney
```

spelling

You aren't sure whether you should use "Webmaster" or "Web master." The term is too recent to appear in the dictionaries at your disposal. In Advanced Search, you select under "As a count only" (instead of "Standard" in the choice of how to display results), and you check the Web for:

```
"web master"
```

and get a score of over 20,000 documents matching the query. Then you try:

```
webmaster
```

and get over 1,000,000. While these numbers are approximate, not precise, you find out that the overwhelming majority of people on the Web use it as one rather than two words.

sports

If you're a sports fan who thinks the world began with ESPN, you're in luck. Just do a Web search for:

```
sports
```

and pick the resources of your choice. Here you'll find lists of links to sports sites where you can read about sports scores, sports figures, and the latest in sports news. However, if you're more selective in your tastes, you can just search out specific sports or teams, as in:

```
football
```

or:

```
Big 12 Basketball
```

On the other hand, you might prefer actively participating to just watching and reading. Try a search for:

```
sports equipment
```

to find dealers and individuals on the Web, or try a Usenet search for something like:

```
golf bag "for sale"
```

standards

If your company is trying to become standards-complaint—which often means being ISO 9000 certified—you'll probably need to bone up on what it all means, as well as trying to figure out how to do it in the most convenient, least painful way. Try a Web search on:

```
ISO 9000
```

If you want to hear the trials and tribulations of people who have already trod the path you're planning, head over to Usenet and search on:

```
ISO 9000 -newsgroups:jobs
```

The *-newsgroups:jobs* eliminates the thousands of jobs being offered to the people familiar with ISO 9000.

substance abuse

Having just had a near collision with a trailer truck on the highway, you are concerned about the issue of substance abuse and truck drivers (he *must* have been on something). You'd like to check to see if federal law requires any kind of drug testing of interstate truck drivers. You do an Advanced Search of the Web for:

```
("substance abuse" OR drug*) AND "truck driver" AND test*
```

and in the ranking box you enter:

```
law interstate federal
```

You get about 200 hits, and right at the top of the list is an article about qualifications necessary to be an interstate truck driver.

If you're looking for information about help for substance abuse, check out "support groups" in this chapter for search ideas.

support groups

Many or most support groups that anyone would ever need are represented on the Internet. Even information for the most obscure support groups is found in Usenet. For example, enter:

```
newsgroups:alt.recovery.clutter
```

if you just cannot keep up with the clutter you keep accumulating. With this search, you'll find links to information on clutter, on containing clutter, on containing your containers, and even on getting rid of your clutter.

Or if your clutter is under control, try searching more globally for:

```
support groups
```

or for:

```
newsgroups:recovery
```

Certainly you can search on the Web for more support group information, like this:

```
"support groups"
```

but it tends to be somewhat less personal than the information on Usenet.

T

tests

If you're approaching the end of a course of education—high school or college—and considering moving on to something bigger and better with presumably higher student loan payments, you'll probably have to take those awful standardized use-a-number-2-pencil-and-bring-two-extras type tests. Color in the circle for AltaVista and search for:

```
standardized tests
```

to get some information about the tests and some preparation programs. For more specific information, try:

```
test preparation courses
```

or something specifically oriented to the test of your choice, such as:

```
LSAT preparation
```

or:

```
SAT preparation
```

In Search of Taxes

In reference to a question about taxes, Steve wrote, among other things:

Finally, if you have access to the World Wide Web, you might find some useful info. I did a search at AltaVista (http://altavista.digital.com) on the topic (using Advanced Search):

> *501(c)3 or 501(c)(3) or 501c3*

sorted by: tax
... and found approximately 4000 entries. At first glance, it appears some of them are useful.
The IRS has a Web site from which you can download its publications and forms, including publications related to 501(c)3 status. The URL is http://www.irs.ustreas.gov/prod/forms_pubs/index.html

Steve Freedkin

---

trademarks

If you're going into business, you might need to check to make sure that your snazzy new product name doesn't infringe on someone else's trademark or registered trademark. These services probably cost some money, but likely less than a lawyer. Look for:

```
"trademark search"
```

and pick the service of your choice.

See also "copyright issues" in this chapter for more search ideas.

travel

So you say you're vacationing in the Cayman Islands? Lucky you! Let AltaVista Search help with your travel plans. For starters, try:

```
Cayman Islands
```

This search gives you about 1000 links to information about the islands as well as tourist attractions. Have you made your hotel reservations yet? Better try a search for:

```
"Cayman Islands" "Holiday Inn"
```

to head directly for the list of Holiday Inns in the islands. You still get over 90 matches with both those terms, many of which can help you plan your visit in some detail before you get there—for instance, comparing a wide variety of scuba diving packages. Then, of course, you need to know what to bring. Check out:

```
"Cayman Islands" weather
```

to see the four-day forecast and also tables of historical information on weather extremes. Better still, search for:

```
+"Cayman Islands" +"rainy season"
```

and you'll discover that the rainy season—with frequent, heavy tropical storms—lasts from May to October. (Whenever you're planning a tropical holiday and counting on lots of sun for outdoor activities, it's a very good idea to do a search for "rainy season" in that locale.)

You can even do newsgroup searches to get candid reactions from vacationers regarding the delights they found and the problems they encountered. For instance:

```
+"Cayman Islands" +problem* vacation
```

gives the paranoid a long list of problems to try to avoid—particularly related to scuba diving. Also, take a look at "weather" in this chapter for more search ideas before leaving for your vacation spot.

In Search of Tools

In reference to a question about finding Morton Machinery on the Web, Jim wrote:

Fundamental Web-browsing 101: Find a good search service—my favorite is Digital's AltaVista: http://altavista.digital.com/—and enter "Morton Machinery" as the query. The very first answer is Morton's Web page, http://www.mortonmachinery.com

Jim Kirkpatrick

---

trivia

If you haven't found enough interesting or bizarre stuff on the Internet yet, just look to the Web for collections of trivia contests with a search for:

```
trivia contest
```

The *Brady Bunch* contest should be a snap for the kids of the '70s, but weather trivia, along with most of the other contests, are fair game for a mixed audience.

If you're specifically interested in contests, check out the search ideas under "contest" in this chapter. Or if you have specific trivial questions, of course, just ask AltaVista Search—someone out there has probably already published the answer!

U

UFO

Need to find out if that blinding light over your house was really a UFO? Read what everyone else has to say about them with a Usenet search for:

```
UFO
```

or possibly for:

```
UFO proof
```

Additionally, a Web search for:

```
+UFO +picture
```

produces a few links with images representing UFOs. Decide for yourself!

urban legends

If you're excited about forwarding that Neiman-Marcus cookie recipe to all your friends, or in a tizzy about the Good Times virus, check out the urban legend information on the Web and Usenet. Specifically, do a Web search for:

```
+"Neiman-Marcus" +debunk*
```

or:

```
+"Good Times" +debunk*
```

For a more comprehensive look at urban legends, check a Web search for:

```
"urban legends"
```

to get the real story behind dozens of hoaxes and bogus stories. Good discussions are also available on the Usenet side of things with the same search. Or you can try:

```
newsgroups:alt.folklore.urban
```

for more focused discussions.

ᘁ

vacation rentals

If you just have to get away from it all but don't really want to stay in a hotel, use either Usenet or the Web to hook up with a vacation rental house. As usual, add the specific location if you want, like this:

```
"vacation rental" +Bahamas
```

But it might just be more fun just to browse (use *"vacation rental"* without the location). Of course, you'll probably need to take care of the pets and houseplants while you're gone, so try:

```
house pet +sitting
```

on both Web and Usenet. With these searches, you'll find loads of ideas for places to leave your pets as well as for services that offer house-sitting while you're gone.

volcano

Natural disasters can be fascinating—if you're far enough away, that is. A search for:

```
volcano
```

gives a whole collection of sites specifically on that subject. If you're looking for information on a specific volcano, just throw the name in as well, like this:

```
volcano "mount saint helens"
```

If you're so fascinated that you just have to seek out an academic program or at least a more scholarly approach to the phenomenon, try:

```
seismology
```

This search provides links to seismology programs at universities, information about plate tectonics, and even simulations.

W

weather

Whether or not you like it, weather is here to stay. If you've just got to have the latest, search for *weather* plus your location, like this:

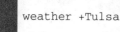

```
weather +Tulsa
```

This search gives you all kinds of choices about the weather information available for the location, ranging from the (fairly) current conditions to the extended forecast. Additionally, you can get the big picture with:

```
weather warnings watches +Tulsa
weather European
"national weather map"
```

or:

```
weather hurricane
```

Certainly, the weather sites cannot replace the accuracy and timeliness of your local forecasters. So, if threatening weather comes along, check out what your local weather guy or gal has to say or turn on weather radio.

Web statistics

Big. How big? BIG! Maybe try something like:

```
measuring "world wide web" marketing +size
```

Or try a site called "Measuring the Web" (searchable by that name), which uses data from AltaVista Search and provides a remarkable picture of the interconnectedness of the Web, if you like that sort of thing.

women's issues

Women's issues and related topics comprise a good-sized chunk of the information available on the Internet. You can start by searching the Web for general information by entering queries like:

```
women's resources
```

or:

```
women's studies
```

With these searches you find everything from resource lists to support groups to public policy information. Similar searches on Usenet tend to be more focused but less productive.

Or you can narrow your search and find specific information. Suppose you are concerned about the issue of female circumcision in Africa and particularly in Ethiopia. Use Advanced Search of both the Web and Usenet, for example:

```
(clitorectomy OR "female circumcision") AND (Africa OR Ethiopia)
```

You get about 200 hits—most of them right on target. Or suppose you would like information regarding sexual harassment in Japan and in Japanese companies. You search the Web for:

```
+"sexual harassment" +Japan*
```

and get about 1000 matches. The top or near-the-top items provide a good overview of the issue.

work

Tired of the old grind? Get up. Shower. Go to work. Work. Go home. Sleep. Get up. Shower. . . Well, AltaVista Search can't bring home the bacon for you, but it can help you find alternatives to your daily grind. If you want to work from home, try a Simple Web Search for:

```
SOHO
```

(yes, use all caps—SOHO stands for Small Office Home Office), or:

```
"alternative officing"
```

which give you links to home officing ideas. Other useful searches would include:

```
telecommuting
```

or possibly:

```
*"health insurance" "self-employ*"
```

world almanac

Oh, come on. You need more information than you can get on the Web? Really? Oh, you say it needs to be portable. In that case, just do a Simple Search for:

```
"world almanac" "book of facts" ordering
```

Of course, a well-directed search for specific information usually suffices. Say you've just got to know the population of South Dakota. No problemo! Try an Advanced Search for:

```
population and ("South Dakota" or SD)
```

and rank by:

```
census bureau
```

X

Xena Warrior Princess

Are you a fan of the syndicated TV series *Xena Warrior Princess* but can't keep track of it because it keeps moving from station to station and time to time? A Simple Search of the Web gets you what you want quickly. Try:

```
+"Xena Warrior Princess" +station*
```

This search gives the time slot (or at least day) and the station of this TV series.

xylography

Huh? You know—xylography—the art of making engravings on wood. If you're interested in some basic information about the art of xylography and its origins, try a Simple Search, like this:

```
xylography
```

Of course, if you can never remember how to spell it, you can always try:

```
wood engraving
```

Y

yachting

OK, so you've had enough of running around with the riffraff. It's time to search for:

```
yachting
```

You can cruise through the links and choose the boat you want to charter. If you're really feeling flush, try:

```
yacht "for sale"
```

See also "weather" in this chapter for more search ideas related to yachting requirements.

yellow pages

Just as the yellow pages in your local phone book let you look before you buy, the yellow pages on the Internet let you do some looking and researching before you buy. Unfortunately, unless there happens to be a set of pages for your area, it's like picking out a set of Yellow Pages from Albany when you live in Boise City. Interesting, but pretty useless. If you're from Albany, try:

```
"yellow pages" +albany
```

Alternatively, if you already know what you're shopping for and haven't been getting enough catalogs in your daily junk mail deliveries, try:

```
catalog
```

You could also search for:

```
catalog -domain:edu
```

to exclude college catalogs—there's rarely anything to buy there.

Z

Zimbabwe

Suppose your company distributes used personal computers and you have heard that there might be good opportunities for sales in Africa, in Zimbabwe in particular.

You'd like to know what the local market is like and would like to find a local company to partner with. You can start with a broad search, like:

```
+Zimbabwe electronics computer*
```

This search yields over 20,000 matches. The country may well be more developed than you imagined. Then, you can focus the search a bit, like this:

```
+Zimbabwe +PC* +used
```

This search gives you over 400 matches, but many of them deal with the question of how to connect to the Internet with a PC from Zimbabwe; and from the country codes, many of the Web sites are in South Africa (.za). You can focus the search even more if you're interested in information that resides directly on servers in Zimbabwe by entering a search with the country code (.zw), like this:

```
+host:zw +PC* +used
```

If you enter the country code, you don't need to enter the country name, in this case Zimbabwe. With this particular search, you get half a dozen matches—all pages at the same server, run by Samara Services. You note the e-mail address of the Webmaster, and you also connect to the root address of the site (stripping away the directory and page portions of the address). From here you can not only get details about the company and its Internet services, but also find useful information about business in Zimbabwe.

zine

Zine (as in maga-zine) is a publication, generally a periodical, about a certain topic. E-zines, as in e-mail, are generally Web-based. Adding +*zine* to a search often brings the zines to the top, as in:

```
cars zine
music zine
```

or:

```
tour* zine
```

zip codes

What businesses and individuals located in a given ZIP code area are on the Internet? Try the Web and Advanced Search (to make it easy to enter all the possible variants of the state name):

```
(MA OR Mass. OR Massachusetts) AND 02132
```

That's the code for West Roxbury, a residential section of Boston, where you would not expect to find many businesses using the Internet. But that search yields over 400 matches—people you might want to get in touch with to share experiences, or possible prospects for services that help companies do business on the Internet, or possible employers. Cool!

zodiac

You can get your daily fix of astrology through a quick Web search for:

```
zodiac
```

and find your way to your horoscope as well as information about the planets in a more prosaic sense. Of course, an Advanced Web search for:

```
(planets or stars or constellation*) AND NOT (movie or film)
```

with:

```
pictures
```

in the ranking field gives you the best view of the stars this side of the *National Enquirer*.

ZOO

Want to take your kids to the zoo but don't want to pile them in the car, wait in lines, or buy cotton candy? Let AltaVista Search take you on a safari! Check out all kinds of animals as well as actual zoos online by searching the Web for:

```
zoo animals
```

They'll see almost as many animals as they could in person. Or try something like:

```
zoo "St. Louis"
```

if you want to visit a specific zoo's Web site. Either way, you'll find an afternoon of fun, lots of information, and even help for the kids' school assignments. Enjoy!

7

The AltaVista Story

The genesis of AltaVista Search—how it was developed and quickly became one of the most widely used and respected Internet resources—is a tale of people, of technology, of innovation, and of many different perspectives on a large and wildly successful project. However, more than anything else, it is a story of synergy. Raging success like AltaVista Search can't just happen, or can it?

SO, WHERE DID ALTAVISTA COME FROM?

The story of AltaVista Search extends far beyond the obvious aspects of software and computers and networks—it ranges into areas such as Digital Equipment Corporation's commitment to research and development and Digital's often altruistic involvement with Internet technology. The serendipitous interaction among the various researchers and their diverse projects combined with Digital's technological advances led to AltaVista Search's development and ultimate success. In turn, the evolution of AltaVista Search created an entire Internet software business that markets and sells not only products and services based on the search technology, but also other Internet software applications as well.

In brief, the synergy among different aspects of Digital Equipment Corporation explains how AltaVista Search grew from a mere proving ground for incredibly fast computers to being the solution to the world's biggest information retrieval problem—the Internet.

AltaVista Search Public Service was not designed to imitate anything that had been done before. While it ultimately shows how Digital is leveraging its expertise in the labs into business solutions, it was not designed with any specific business model in mind. To the researchers who developed AltaVista Search, the main purpose was to do what many considered impossible. The researchers needed to explore their ideas and push the limits of performance as far as possible and see where that would take them. Only after this new creation was a proven success did the business people start to look into a variety of marketable applications for the technology.

The AltaVista Search story provides the background and sets the stage for these interactions and describes the technology, the network, the programs, the people, and the project that led to the product now known as AltaVista Search Public Service. The story concludes—but really just begins—with the next generation of AltaVista Search and the exciting business possibilities that have evolved with it.

SETTING THE STAGE

AltaVista Search resulted from Digital Equipment Corporation's investment in research, emphasis on the Internet, and business attitude toward research and applied technology. The investments and commitments that eventually yielded the program grew from the development of the Palo Alto research labs, the ongoing emphasis on Internet-related technology, and from a business approach that emphasized effective and quick use of innovative developments.

DIGITAL ON RESEARCH

Over the past twenty years, Digital's research endeavors have evolved into a much more structured and organized approach than was originally practiced. In the 1970s and '80s, when industrial research first became a prominent part of large corporations, the Digital model fostered creativity in the form of pure research, without particular regard for business needs. The approach was to "gather very bright people, give them the best possible environment, then sit back and wait for magic to happen," notes Bob Supnik, vice president in charge of research at Digital.

Sam Fuller, the vice president who built the company's research organization, notes, "Back then, Digital was at the stage in its growth where it needed applied research capabilities second to none in the industry. We invested to develop our capabilities in important applied research areas to make sure we were at the forefront of computing."

As the Information Technology industry matured, Digital's research program moved from a model of undirected industrial research toward research based on market and business needs. The transition has attempted to preserve innovation while maintaining a focus on the marketplace and the corporation.

Digital now focuses—like most other corporate R&D shops—on applied research. Rather than just retreating into labs to conduct research for its own sake, researchers must focus their efforts on applying innovative concepts to solving engineering problems. According to Bill Strecker, Vice President and Chief Technical Officer in charge of corporate strategy and technology, "Research efforts must now have a practical realization to help the company develop, grow, and compete. Practical research, of course, requires that the research efforts actually result in a tangible product, so the researchers also build, use, and evaluate experimental prototypes."

This process is precisely what led to the development of AltaVista Search. The use of a research and development approach, sheltering the developers from the daily scrutiny of business units, made it possible for the AltaVista Search team to complete a prototype very quickly. It was less than six months from the time the researchers started to the time that AltaVista Search went live on the Internet and started serving millions of users. The first research investigations into very large memory indexes quickly led to investigations on retrieving and indexing immense amounts of information from the Web and finally led to the initial public unveiling of AltaVista Search in December 1995.

The resulting success heralded the development of commercial applications of the AltaVista Search software technology and services. Today, AltaVista Internet Software, Inc., sells search software for intranets along with all types of Internet-related software including firewalls, tunneling, mail, conferencing, and directories. All of which just goes to show that emphasizing research and development—even in unconventional ways—can have an enormous impact on a company or a product.

The very short time-to-market that the sheltered research environment made possible was essential to the success of AltaVista Search because the Internet changes so quickly. If it took an extra year to develop useful capabilities, by the time they were ready, the needs probably would have changed. As it is, AltaVista Search today provides such a useful service that Webmasters go out of their way to make sure their sites can be found and indexed.

PIONEERING THE INTERNET

Researchers at Digital's Palo Alto Lab have been involved with the Internet from its earliest days. They frequently work in partnership with other Internet pioneers and have a tradition of doing whatever they can to help the Internet thrive. By way of example, for over ten years the Labs have maintained one of the world's largest archives of free public software, available for anyone to download over the Internet at any time. Additionally, the Palo Alto Labs serve as a major news backbone for the Internet.

In fact, Digital claims a lot of firsts on the Internet that—looking back—are quite impressive. Did you know that Digital

- was the first Fortune 500 company to establish a public Web server?

- established the first Internet presence for a city in America? (Palo Alto, California)

- was the first computer company with an ARPAnet (the original Internet) site?

- was the first organization anywhere in the world to have two geographically separate gateways (in Massachusetts and California)?

And there's more! Did you know that Digital

- was the world's first computer company to register an Internet domain?

- created the world's first corporate Internet mail gateway?

- created the world's first commercial Internet print server?

We aren't done yet! Did you know that Digital

- is a founding member of the World Wide Web Consortium?

- was one of the first company's to utilize public USENET Newsgroups for customer support?

- was the first computer company to offer online ordering over the Internet?

- even today has one of the most active gateways in the Internet?

OK. Enough bragging, but you get the picture. Far from being a flash in the pan, AltaVista Search is merely the latest in a long line of Digital's Internet projects as well as the latest in the services provided to the Internet community.

One of the predecessors to AltaVista Search was a marketing endeavor from October 1993. As soon as Web browsers became available for PCs, the Palo Alto researchers made Digital's marketing information available on the World Wide Web. Thus Digital became the one of the first Fortune 500 companies to actively use the Web for marketing, clearly demonstrating the business potential of the increasingly Web-centric Internet, while benefiting the corporation at the same time.

A series of "Internet showcase" projects soon followed this pioneer use of the Internet. These practical experiments used the World Wide Web to show the potential of that new medium, to assess what technology it would take to be effective, and to evaluate the business implications of the technology.

Early in 1994, the Palo Alto research team made theirs first city on the Web. Later that year, the researchers took on the enormous task of providing live coverage of the California state election on the Internet. In addition to providing the basic won-lost tallies, the team generated detailed graphics of results in all parts of the state on the fly—as quickly as the information was entered into the computers. Maps and graphs of the results were also available through the site. That project clearly demonstrated the importance of the Internet for government and for elections in particular, and also pushed the limits of available technology in serving hundreds of thousands of users in a concentrated period of time, delivering not just text but complex graphical material to all those users, and doing so with excellent response, even at times of peak usage.

These and other projects were not sales efforts by Digital. Rather, they were attempts to gain direct practical experience and to break new ground on the Web, and, not incidentally, to move the Internet a giant step ahead toward being a practical medium for marketing, sales, government, and a wide variety of business endeavors.

Researchers like Brian Reid and other Internet pioneers at Digital saw that the Internet was the future of computing and communication, that it would transform how people and companies work and interact. They thought that in the long run, in ways that might not be immediately apparent, doing what's best for the Internet would be a sensible approach from a business perspective as well. They were right.

Building a Showcase

The AltaVista Search Public Service actually began in the spring of 1995. Louis Monier, a researcher from Digital's Western Research Lab, was talking over lunch to Joella Paquette, a marketing specialist in Digital's Internet Business Group. Paul Flaherty, from Digital's Network Systems Lab, joined them, and the rest, as they say, is history.

Paul Flaherty knew from personal experience that finding information on the Web was becoming increasingly difficult. It seemed that the Internet's usefulness would be soured by sheer information overload and complexity. Paul had an ambitious idea about how to demonstrate Digital's newest product, the Alpha 8400 (TurboLaser)—a computer that in tests had shown it could run database software a hundred times faster than the competition. "That was spectacular," he recalls. "You don't normally see that kind of leap in technology—two orders of magnitude in performance."

It dawned on Paul that a database could be used for Internet search and that a machine a hundred times faster than anything else at database applications could do a much better job of searching than anyone had ever done. Paul wanted to build a database of the Web and provide access to it as a free service to everyone on the Internet.

Keying off this idea, Louis Monier envisioned a *full text* search of the Web, with every word from every page at every site available to searchers. According to Joella, "As the team explored this idea, it fueled our enthusiasm the more and more we talked. It sounded like a natural winner—likely to attract millions of users per day."

As so often happens in a research environment, one great idea leads to more great ideas, and so came the notion of making the whole Web searchable.

Scooter

The software needed to search and automatically find and bring back information about Web pages—fast enough for the information to be current—hadn't been developed. This software would have to operate at unprecedented speeds of up to a hundred times faster than anything currently available and would have to retrieve millions of pages per day.

Programs that automatically visit Web sites and gather information are variously known as "spiders," "crawlers," "robots,", or "agents," because they crawl around the Web looking for data. A program intended to visit not just a few select sites, but rather every page on the entire public Web—tens of millions of pages—would have to operate at extraordinary speed to bring back pages fast enough for the information to be timely.

To appreciate the complexity of the problem, consider that a "spider" functions very much like a browser. Imagine that you set out with a browser and clicked to a site and jotted down what you saw and checked to see if you had seen it before. Then you clicked on another link and another link, each time checking to see if it was new. It would take time to get to each page and more time to get links to sites you

7

Comments from the Inside: Philip Steffora

"I inherited a growing baby with a voracious appetite for TurboLasers," remarks Philip Steffora, AltaVista's Operations Manager. "When I joined AltaVista in April 1996, we were rolling the third and allegedly 'final' TurboLaser in the door. Five months later, we expect delivery very soon of four additional TurboLasers, bringing our current total to eleven.

"AltaVista has provided remarkable operational challenges for my team. We have now automated much of the monitoring and troubleshooting, leaving our late nights available for continued expansion and hardware installation. Not a week goes by that we don't add at least one new server or major piece of hardware. Our goals for the future include continuing to increase performance, reliability, and redundancy, while working to satisfy the ravenous hunger for more hardware."

hadn't been to before. And if you built a program that went through those same operations, nonstop, twenty-four hours a day, it might only get about a page a minute, or fewer than 1500 pages a day. At that rate, it would take such a program more than a human lifetime to look at 30 million pages just once.

So Louis Monier, leading the project with a team of experienced Internet, software, networking, and hardware experts inside Digital's research labs, developed Scooter, the super-spider. Scooter was created from scratch with the sole intention of making AltaVista Search Public Service a reality. Louis's team not only produced Scooter in remarkably short time but also developed the Web front-end for Scooter and the indexing software that millions of people now know as AltaVista Search.

How Can It Work So Fast?

AltaVista Search produces results remarkably quickly—it's actually probably faster to find something on the Internet through AltaVista Search than it is to find something right on your personal computer through more conventional means. Part of the reason for the difference is, of course, the AltaVista Search software itself. However, the hardware that runs AltaVista Public Search—the query interface, Scooter, and the indexing software—is pretty impressive as well.

The Query Interface, what you see at **http://altavista.digital.com/** and probably think of as *being* AltaVista Search, runs on a set of three Digital Equipment Corporation AlphaStations—three AlphaStation 500/333s, each with 256MB of RAM and 4GB of hard disk space. Each of these systems runs a custom multi-threaded Web server that accepts your queries and sends the queries along to the index servers. These systems, relatively small by AltaVista Search standards, forward millions of hits per day to the AltaVista Search index servers, with roughly 90 percent of the queries going to the Web and the remaining 10 percent to newsgroups.

The real basis for AltaVista Search's superior performance is a set of seven AlphaServer 8400 5/300 systems, each with ten processors, 6GB of RAM, and 210GB of hard disk in a RAID array. (RAID systems are sets of hard disks that work together and ensure that if a hard disk fails, no information is lost.) Each server holds a complete copy of the Web index (currently 40GB) and provides response times of less than a second.

Scooter runs on a AlphaServer 4100 with 1GB RAM and a 48GB RAID array. All Scooter has to do is roam the Web, retrieve information, and send it to the indexing system, which compiles the index. An AlphaServer 600 with 256MB RAM, two processors, and 1GB of memory, actually builds the index, and then copies it to the index servers.

The news server runs on an AlphaServer 600 system, with 256MB of RAM and 24GB of RAID hard disk. This server keeps the news articles spool for the News Indexer and serves the articles to users who want to read news with their standard Web browser. The News Indexer runs on an AlphaServer 600 system, with 256MB of RAM and 13GB of hard disk. This machine maintains an up-to-date index of the news spool, which includes handling the constant turnover of thousands of news articles as some expire and are deleted and others arrive in the system.

A Database or an Index?

Even with the help of Scooter to retrieve all of the Web pages and pour them into a database, getting results back out again would be a challenge. Developing a database would require a very large computer application that could record key bits of information about every Web page on the Internet. With such an enormous amount of data to search through—that is, data about everything on the Web—if people made simple one-word queries using keywords, they'd get many thousands of responses, which would not necessarily be useful. In addition, there was no way that a database approach could provide the fast response users would require.

Fortunately, software for an alternative approach—high-speed full-text indexing—had been developed by another researcher in Palo Alto. The indexing software seemed a good match—the only challenge was that the index would require that the *entire Internet*, for all intents and purposes, be reproduced on computers at the Palo Alto labs. Digital's indexing software started out humbly as a way to organize e-mail, and then, because it worked so well, evolved to an indexing system for the newsgroups.

The experience with these earlier projects helped the researchers understand, despite conventional wisdom to the contrary, that indexing the entire Web might be feasible. The indexing software was overhauled at about the time that the AltaVista Search Public Service project was taking off, and the huge set of data that Scooter was retrieving from the Web proved to be the perfect test of the new software.

A rough estimate indicated that all the text on the entire Web probably amounted to less than one terabyte (a thousand gigabytes). In other words, the Web wasn't quite monstrous beyond imagination—every single word could be indexed, which would make the new search engine far more powerful and useful than anything else in existence. Additional work was needed so the indexer could handle the tens of millions of pages of text on the Web fast enough, but the target was within range. Although the rest of the world continued to think that a true complete index of every word on the Web was, for practical purposes, impossible, Louis and the team knew that, despite the difficulty, it could be done with off-the-shelf computer hardware and their own custom indexing software.

So within a few weeks after beginning work on this project, the AltaVista Search team changed their approach from a classification system using keywords in a database to building a full text index of the entire Internet. The indexer would be far faster and far more powerful than a database, able to search for complete phrases and sentences and to link words in complex queries at no loss of speed. (Leaping tall buildings is currently in beta test.) And the AltaVista Search team would manage the anarchic, unstructured information of the Internet by using a tool that had been designed for dealing with large masses of unstructured information—a perfect match.

How Does the Indexer Work?

First, the indexing software takes the text of a document and examines every word in it to create an index organized by word. It saves each instance of each word along with the URL of the page on which it appears, and information about its location in that document. That level of detail is necessary in order to do phrase searches, which depend on knowing the exact order of all the words within a document.

It indexes all instances of a word, regardless of capitalization, as lowercase, and additionally indexes all words with capitalization again, exactly as their typography indicates. That allows users to do a general search or to narrow the search for unique capitalization, as in trademarks.

Similarly, it indexes under the English letter equivalent all instances of words with accented letters from non-English languages that use Latin characters. Once again, at the cost of enlarging the index, this approach gives users considerable flexibility in focusing their searches.

In addition, no order is imposed on this enormous body of information to make it accessible. AltaVista Search simply indexes words. It takes the unstructured content of the Internet and, without adding some arbitrary or human-designed structure or categorization, makes it easy for users to find what they want.

Making It Happen

Once the decision was made to use the indexer, Louis took charge of the project. He was very excited, even messianic about AltaVista Search. He got lots of people in the Labs involved, soliciting suggestions and criticisms. Louis notes that he "started from scratch," with no knowledge of networks. However, the top people in the field were readily available right there at the Labs, and he could drop in on them at any time and ask about any aspect of the Internet or the Web or HTML—the text markup language used to create Web pages. He could get a "brain dump" from those experts and in a few hours know what he needed to know, or ask a targeted question and get the answer right away.

Glenn Trewitt and Stephen Stuart, researchers from the Network Systems Lab, were part of the core team that provided the networking expertise, designing the networks and putting together the hardware needed to run AltaVista Search Service. With their experience in network design and topology mapping, they set out to ensure that AltaVista Search would have the hardware and network connectivity needed for a successful debut. (Stephen administers Digital's showcase Internet gateway in Palo Alto.) Before the AltaVista Search launch, the connectivity was somewhat over ten million bits per second—probably not enough to handle the load when AltaVista

Search's customers showed up on launch day. With just a few months' warning, Stephen, Glenn, and others worked to upgrade Digital's connection to the Internet to over 135 million bits per second by the day of the launch. And this has grown even more since AltaVista Search appeared on the scene.

Whenever Louis needed equipment, which happened frequently, he could go to the system administrator, Annie Warren, and ask for a spare machine. And repeatedly she was able to come up with what he needed. Research facilities don't budget exactly for what people expect they'll need. The unexpected happens all the time, so spares are set aside for projects such as these.

"Remember," notes Annie, "we did this while running at full speed. We've never had the luxury of saying, 'This is what we're going to do. This is what we'll need. Now let's order the hardware for it.' We've always been doing a hundred or two hundred percent more than we ever thought we could with the hardware and trying to retrofit everything so we can eke out that tiny little bit more. We've been doing the equivalent of fine-tuning a race car engine while it is in the race."

Piece by piece, Annie gave Louis all her hoarded just-in-case equipment. Additionally, many of the researchers provided spare systems or memory cards to give Louis the hardware he needed.

Louis emphasizes that Digital's Labs was probably the only place in the world where this work could get done so quickly. No startup company could afford the research staff. No university could have afforded the investment in equipment. And other large companies have not consistently invested in research the way Digital has.

So What's an Alpha? Where's the Omega?

AltaVista Search Public Service runs exclusively on Digital Equipment Corporation Alpha computers—albeit several of them. Two main characteristics provide the exceptional performance that AltaVista Search users tend to take for granted—64-bit architecture and incredible amounts of memory. For the specifics, read on!

Architecture of the Future

"AltaVista is the problem Alpha was designed to solve. It demonstrates the capabilities that were built into the architecture back in 1988-89."
—*Bob Supnik, Vice President, Digital Research Laboratories*

Alpha computers use something called a 64-bit architecture, which is a key factor in their performance. In contrast, most common personal computers today use 32-bit architecture, and often use software designed for 16-bit systems.

The number of bits designates how large a "word" the computer can handle at once. If everything else is equal, bigger words yield better performance. If the computer does a specific number of calculations per second but can consider more information per calculation, the performance improves. (It's exactly the same reason that firefighters use great big hoses instead of garden hoses—they can get more water through a bigger pipe.)

Alpha systems use 64-bit words—a very large pipe—which increases performance in many AltaVista operations, particularly calculating and comparing the information necessary to perform phrase and proximity searches. Additionally, using 64-bit words dramatically improves the way Alpha computers store and retrieve information, resulting in proportionate improvements in performance. If a typical query takes .2 seconds instead of 20 seconds, a search engine is transformed from being a curiosity to being a reliable, everyday tool.

Ten years ago, 32 bits were quite sufficient, even for high-end computers, because the amounts of information that computers were called upon to manage were far less than they are today. To handle tasks involving many gigabytes and even terabytes (a thousand times bigger than a gigabyte) of information requires the extra capacity and power of a 64-bit machine. And as an even greater proportion of the world's information is stored in digital form and made accessible over the Internet, computer systems will need to address, manage, and process petabytes of information (a thousand times bigger than a terabyte)—still well within the capabilities of 64-bit architecture.

Memories

"AltaVista shows the practical value of machines that have more than 4 gigabytes of physical main memory."
—Dick Sites, Digital Equipment Corporation Systems Research Lab

In addition to 64-bit architecture, AltaVista Search Alpha computer systems also use large amounts of memory, which helps improve the speed of your searches. Computers store information in two forms: the main memory (RAM), which is extremely fast and readily available for processing; and disk storage, which is about ten thousand times slower but is much less expensive and has much larger capacity. Computers that hold more information in RAM perform better than those that hold less information, if everything else is equal.

High performance, which is essential given the demands placed on AltaVista Search, requires holding as much information as possible in main memory—preferably the information that is most frequently used, so the system doesn't have to waste time fetching new items from disk. To get a sense of the relative size of the RAM in AltaVista Search, consider that a typical personal computer today comes with 8 to 16MB of RAM, and the AltaVista Index Servers each have 6GB of RAM—about 500 times more.

With 6GB of memory each, the AltaVista Index Servers can hold in main memory large chunks of the index—including document descriptors such as title, URL, and abstract. That means far fewer disk accesses and hence machines that can provide fast service to millions more people per day than would be possible with less RAM.

BUILDING THE PROTOTYPE

The seed of the idea that became AltaVista Search was planted in April 1995. By June, Louis was writing the code for the spider—Scooter. Meanwhile, work was proceeding on the indexer, fine-tuning that software in anticipation of an enormous new set of data that would soon be coming, and scaling up the performance by a factor of ten to accommodate the amount of information Scooter would retrieve.

The challenge in building Scooter was figuring out how to get lots of documents very quickly. They needed to be able to fetch the text of the entire Web quickly enough so information in the index would be reasonably current. The solution was using a "multi-threaded" program—the equivalent of having a thousand people browse the Web simultaneously. But that led to complexities in coordinating the activities of a thousand threads, all launched from one machine and one program, and taking all steps to maximize performance.

Because the Internet is so unstructured and so many people who create Web pages don't follow all the standards for documents, Louis couldn't precisely predict performance without live trials. There was no way to imagine all the myriad of complexities that Scooter would encounter. Louis had to design and redesign, time and again throughout the summer.

Scooter's first few limited trials occurred in June 1995. Over the Fourth of July weekend, Louis released Scooter to begin its first big crawl. Louis wanted to be sure that his creation didn't bother too many people before he'd had a chance to perfect it, and that weekend is typically a low-traffic time on the Internet because so much of the Internet is still based in the United States. Louis started with a few URLs and let Scooter loose. At that point, Louis was running with a limited number of threads and constantly experimenting with the code to optimize performance.

"With a spider, if you have a bug, no matter how small, you are going to hear about it a lot because your spider will affect a lot of sites," observes Louis. "When you use multiple threads, that's like launching many different spiders at the same time, and your code is soon very visible to the whole planet. That reality forced on me a sense of responsibility that I've never had before." In order not to harass or trouble people, Louis built special safeguards into Scooter as well as obeying all conventions, such as the Robot Exclusion Standard. In other words, Scooter checks a special file at each Web site before visiting any of its pages. This file may contain a list of directories and pages that the site's Webmaster does not want robot programs to visit. Scooter does not fetch any of those. (See Chapter 5 for more information about controlling what Scooter visits.)

By the end of August 1995, Louis was ready for a big, full-scale crawl, and this time Scooter brought back about ten million pages. This experiment and the previous ones confirmed the estimate that the Web was not quite the monster that others thought it was. Extrapolations from what Scooter had found indicated that the Web probably consisted of over 80,000 servers and over thirty million indexable documents, with the average document containing just five kilobytes (the equivalent of a couple of pages of printed text). Later, when the system went into production mode and Scooter was allowed to search farther, these estimates were refined upward to over 200,000 servers and about fifty million Web pages—but that was still in the same order of magnitude. In other words, as they had suspected, a full-text index of the entire Web was small enough to be manageable. Suddenly, the future of the Internet and how people would use it looked very different.

7

Piping Information into the Internet

"We don't so much connect to the Internet, as we have it in our living room."

—Stephen Stuart, Researcher, Digital Equipment Corporation

For the AltaVista Public Search Service to maintain consistently high levels of performance and serve millions of users per day requires not just powerful computer hardware, but also extremely fast Internet access. Fortunately, even before AltaVista Search's appearance on the scene, Digital already had an enormous "pipe" coming from the Internet into the Network Systems Laboratory in Palo Alto, California.

When you're talking about networks, the unit of measure you use is megabits (millions of bits) carried per second. An average company might lease a T1 line from a telecommunications company, which provides a "bandwidth" of about 1.5 megabits per second, and in many cases could be enough to meet the needs of an entire company. Very large companies and those that resell Internet service to other companies might lease a T3 line, which provides about 45 megabits per second. T3 is the standard for building a serious, continental-size network. Digital Equipment Corporation's Palo Alto Labs connect to the Internet at more than twice that speed with 100 megabits per second (using technology known as "switched FDDI") into the routers of all their Internet service providers.

THE PITCH!

On September 29, 1995, Louis made a presentation to corporate management on the East Coast, pointing out that at that time the search services on the Internet were either a table of contents based on manual classification, or a "back-of-the-book" index based on selected keywords. He explained that AltaVista Search would explore the Web, find and fetch each page, read the contents of each page, find all the words, and add them to an index that would be accessible throughout the Internet.

One index would hold every word for the entire Web. Scooter could fetch pages at a rate more than a hundred times faster than anything then available. The full-text indexing software could index these pages as fast as Scooter could fetch them and provide a complete representation of all the text on the Web. It could very quickly handle queries that included phrases, complex combinations of terms, and unique structural elements of Web and newsgroup articles. And it would rank matches, so pages that were most likely to be useful would appear at the top of the list.

Louis emphasized the value to Digital of creating the "ultimate" Web indexing site and described an internal pilot he was already rolling out for use by Digital employees. He was shooting for December 15, 1995, as a public launch date.

As a result of this presentation, the project became highly visible throughout the company. How would the world react to the AltaVista Search Public Service? How would they view it compared with other Internet search services? What should be done to ensure the success of AltaVista Search? What was the marketing plan? How could this service generate revenue? What about related services?

While there were many questions to finalize, lots of enthusiasm and support came from all over the company to help AltaVista Search's launch in the form of hardware, planning and marketing and communications expertise. According to Jay Zager, finance manager for Digital's Advanced Technology Group, "the competitive advantage was clear, as was the need to move quickly. After all, on the Internet, extraordinary change can take place in a matter of days, and startup companies are legendary for their rapid response." Digital could not afford to follow its ordinary business procedures in this case. They needed to position this project so it could move ahead with a minimum of hassle and delay.

In fact, the company had just announced its corporate strategy to the press and analysts, and the Internet was an important part of that strategy. But in the marketplace, even with all of its pioneering Internet history, Digital was still not perceived as a major Internet player. Sharon Henderson, then communications director for the Advanced Technology Group, recalls, "Digital had been in the Internet business for years, but I could call up any press person at a major publication and they couldn't tell me what Digital was doing on the Internet. The problem was that our servers and software were used in the back room. They weren't things that end users could touch and feel. Here was an opportunity to reach the broadest possible audience. My goal was to make sure that the message didn't just go to people who already understood the Internet, but also my grandmother or my father who could use it. In terms of visibility, this could be the biggest announcement that Digital had ever made."

So instead of quietly releasing the technology to the Internet user community, Sharon pushed for bringing in the big guns from corporate public relations and making a major announcement in the press. The decision was made to stick with the December 15 launch date.

7

The Internal Pilot

While preparing for that management presentation, Louis and the team were also getting the internal pilot up and running. They fed the ten million pages that Scooter had found to the indexer and then provided a search service for Digital employees as a live test of the capability. The pilot lasted for about two months and involved about 10,000 employees, who posted an average of about 10,000 total queries per day. Now, as internal testing proceeded, the developers had to deal not just with the diversity of the unstructured Web content, but also with the diversity of behavior and preferences of 10,000 individuals at Digital, many of whom were quite vocal and very helpful in making their preferences known.

This internal testing turned up a number of bugs with the user interface, most of which involved compatibility with a plethora of existing Web browsers. The development team struggled to understand why particular browsers repeatedly had trouble with certain features.

It was at this stage that the AltaVista Search development team decided to include both "Simple" and "Advanced" Search. Simple would be an intuitive search format allowing users to pose queries in plain language—any Western language—and immediately get useful results. Advanced, on the other hand, would be the native query language of the indexing software, using the terms of Boolean logic, such as *and* and *or*, which many technically-oriented people are already familiar with.

"AltaVista" was the code name for the project. Now that AltaVista Search was going public, much discussion went into deciding if the name and graphics were correct. It is a little-known fact outside Digital that until two days prior to the launch of AltaVista Search Public Service, the name and graphics were going to be completely different from the AltaVista Search that millions of Internet users know today. One of the early recommendations made by Ilene Lang, president of what is now known as AltaVista Internet Software, Inc., was to keep the AltaVista name.

So What's in a Name?

OK, is it Alta Vista, AltaVista, or AltaVista Search? Once the popularity of AltaVista Search (the public service on the WWW) became apparent, Digital quickly realized the opportunities for branding a business under the AltaVista name. So here goes the name game:

- AltaVista Internet Software, Inc., is the business that owns and runs the search engine and sells software products and services based on the search technology. (They also sell other Internet software such as firewalls, tunneling, mail, conferencing, and directories.)

- AltaVista Search is the line of products and services based on the search technology.

- AltaVista Search Public Service is the Internet search engine.

- AltaVista Search World Wide Network Affiliates are mirror sites of the Internet search engine.

- AltaVista Search Business eXtension is a service to content providers and Web sites like Yahoo! that utilize the technology and power of the Internet search engine to run Web searches from their own Web sites.

- AltaVista Search Private eXtensions are the products based on the Internet search engine that are used in corporate intranets—AltaVista Search for Intranets, for Workgroups, and for My Computer.

Meanwhile, another internal pilot project at Digital demonstrated the value of an AltaVista Search Service for *intranets*. Intranets are corporate networks that use Internet networking technology and techniques to deliver information to and interact with employees and selected suppliers, customers, and partners in a secure, closed environment. These networks use hardware and software products known as *firewalls* and *tunnels* to block out intruders and facilitate confidential communications among trusted parties.

Digital's intranet is used by all of the company's 60,000 employees. It was originally assumed that there were about 300 internal Web servers—which seemed like an enormous number compared to the few external Web servers that the company used to deliver information to the public. Running an intranet version of Scooter and AltaVista Search, the company discovered that they in fact had over 1100 internal servers and over 900,000 Web pages. AltaVista Search would not only make this information far more accessible to the people who needed it, but also show AltaVista Search's value as a diagnostic tool—helping companies better understand how Internet technology is used internally and helping them to make better use of their computing resources.

"The value of data appears to be greater the more of it you have," Brian Reid, head of Digital's Western Research Lab adds. "If you get twice as much data, it has more than twice the value. The increase in value is greater than linear simply because of the higher the probability that you will find what you are looking for, and the greater likelihood that you will ask in the first place. A library that only has a hundred books is not worth going to. A library that has every known book is always worth going to. And the more information it has, the more valuable it is in proportion to the actual amount of information. So AltaVista Search, by enabling you to find things, increases the value of the information that you have on file."

Comments from the Inside: Annie Warren

"So much of what we do in research goes into high-level design that's invisible to most people," she reflects. "Now it's fun to work on something that you and your friends and relatives can personally use and enjoy. I got my dad to buy a PC after he used AltaVista. I got another friend to actually sign up for an Internet account, someone who is not computer literate at all, but she does genealogical searches. I brought her here to the office and showed her; and all of a sudden, she needed a PC and an account with an Internet service provider. Now she spends all her days doing genealogical searches using AltaVista instead of making her annual pilgrimage to Utah to stand there at books looking through birth records. It's so much fun for me to be able to say to my friends who are not in the computer industry, 'Look, this is what we do, and you'll really like it.'"

THE LAUNCH!

On December 15, 1995, AltaVista Search was open to the public. The team working on AltaVista Search saw the launch as an experiment. If it was successful, there were enormous product and service possibilities based on the search technology.

The launch was *very* successful. Usage grew dramatically— from 300,000 hits on the first day to over nineteen million a day nine months later. Early users returned again and again and quickly spread the word about its many possible uses. Thousands of articles appeared in newsgroups of all kinds telling of individual experiences and sharing the enthusiasm of discovery. Awards and stories from all over the planet began to flood newspapers and magazines about AltaVista Search. Finally, anyone who had access to a Web browser had an easy way to find information on the Internet.

The Birth of a New Business

On May 7, 1996, AltaVista Search had another launch of sorts. The AltaVista Internet Software business unit was launched in a worldwide event hosted by Bob Palmer, Digital's president and CEO; Ilene Lang, the new business unit's vice president; and Louis Monier. Essentially, what Digital decided to do was to brand a number of its Internet- related software products under the AltaVista name and brand the software technology behind the search engine "AltaVista Search."

The event, billed as "The AltaVista CyberCast," took place in physical and virtual space and reached every corner of the globe. The physical host setting was the CyberSmith café in Harvard Square, Cambridge, Massachusetts, a drop-in center/computer store normally frequented by patrons who pay per minute to sit at computer screens and use the Internet while sipping coffee and munching snacks. The virtual site was hosted via **http://altavista.software.digital.com**, the newly developed and itself innovative Web site supporting Digital's AltaVista Internet Software product business. Customers, investment analysts, and press gathered in New York City, Paris, Valbonne, Rotterdam, London, and Stockholm could see the speakers present material and answer questions. In addition the Web site, accessed by hundreds of thousands of users, multicast the event using audio and video.

What those participants saw and heard was an unfolding of the business plan, dramatized by the new AltaVista Internet Software products themselves and focused on new search software technology developed for intranets. Bob Palmer set the tone for the event in his opening remarks, declaring that Digital is continuing its tradition of innovation with the launch of a business unit that will help build the new computing paradigm of the twenty-first century—the Internet! Next, Ilene Lang highlighted the AltaVista product portfolio (including versions of AltaVista Search for personal computers, workgroups, and intranets), outlined the business plan, and announced plans to franchise mirror sites of the AltaVista Search Service—all to accelerate and proactively shape the future of both Internet and intranet computing.

7

EXTENDING SUCCESS

Where does the AltaVista Search go from here? With the tremendous growth in popularity of the single AltaVista Search Public Service in Palo Alto, California, the natural course of action is to deliver more of a good thing by mirroring the AltaVista Search Public Service site in many geographically dispersed locations throughout the world. In fact, AltaVista Search has already set up two sites with Telia in Sweden and Telestra/Yellow Pages in Australia. C/Net, the Web's leading technical news and software source, provides similar AltaVista services to its users. AltaVista Search is becoming the de facto standard search service on the Internet.

In addition, AltaVista Search Public Service also now offers Webmasters a version of AltaVista Search that allows visitors to a site to search the Web using the AltaVista Search engine without actually having to link to the AltaVista Search home page. Yahoo!, one of the Internet's first guides, is a good example: Yahoo! users' searches are now powered by AltaVista Search software whenever they want to search the Web.

Where else can AltaVista Search go? As a result of the visibility and usefulness that Internet technologies have brought to the public arena, many corporations are recognizing the value of adopting the same capabilities inside their operations on their intranets. Many have set up networks using the same technology as the Internet and are installing standard Web browsers on computers to provide access to corporate information. As the number of corporate intranet Web pages grows ever more rapidly, businesses will find that spending time just pursuing information is not as productive as using that information.

The researchers and business people decided that putting technology behind the Internet search engine to work for today's corporations, universities, and government agencies would be tremendously helpful. Thus, AltaVista Search Private eXtensions were born. (*Note*: If you are on the Internet, you are using the "public" extension to the Search Service. If you are using a version of AltaVista Search behind a firewall on a private network, you are using the "private" eXtension of AltaVista Search Public Service.) AltaVista Search Private eXtensions extend the public search engine technology to private business environments, slightly adapted for locating various types of useful information on corporate intranets, personal desktops, or any file server a desktop is connected to—in seconds.

In fact, in July 1996, an early release of a desktop version of AltaVista Search Private eXtension was made available for free trial downloading over the Internet: AltaVista Search—My Computer Private eXtension. Imagine being able to instantly find data buried in an old e-mail message or finding a file you thought was lost—accidentally saved deep in an obscure directory. With this tool, you can preserve all your work without complicated filing and naming systems and directories, and without worrying about how you'll be able to find it later. This version makes it possible to find information on your own computer as easily as you can over the Web, with the same AltaVista Search look and feel and same commands. Other versions of AltaVista Search have been released also. To find out the latest and greatest (and even get some free beta software), check out the AltaVista Internet Software, Inc. "MarketSpace" at **http://altavista.software.digital.com**.

THE ALTAVISTA REVOLUTION CONTINUES ...

The AltaVista Search Public Service has spawned a new vision of the Internet, providing a higher view from which to locate and access valuable resources. And it has inspired broader use of Internet technologies across the enterprise and around the world. Digital is building on the success of the AltaVista Search Public Service, with a business focused on an entire family of software products, AltaVista Internet Software, Inc. Using Internet technology as a common, ubiquitous environment, AltaVista Internet Software provides users with dynamic, global capabilities for exchanging information and ideas.

The AltaVista Search Public Service is truly revolutionary in scope, breaking through traditional barriers that limit communication and information access. AltaVista Search is both a vision and a reality, offering immediate rewards even as it inspires new, innovative technology. AltaVista Search is the key that unlocks all the Internet has to offer.

7

The Top 1,000
Most Common
Words on the
World Wide Web

A list of the 1,000 most common words on the World Wide Web reflects the university and computer science origins of the Internet. The top nouns found include: information, page, net, home, index, data, system, and university. The numbers shown here are for comparison only—they keep changing (and getting larger) whenever Scooter, the AltaVista Search spider, combs the Web for pages, but the order of the words tends to stay relatively stable.

HOW TO SEARCH MOST EFFECTIVELY

When you use AltaVista Search to search for something, it is important to keep in mind that the words listed in the table below are common—meaning they are found in a great number of documents—and including them in your search command may not be very useful, since so many Web pages contain these words. Imagine if you had to look up a word in a dictionary and your only clue was that it had the word "and" in the description. The same principles apply to AltaVista Search. If your searches contain only very common words, your search results will turn up a large number of hits that may not be very useful to you. When you can, it helps to use rare, or not-so-common, words in your searches.

Here are some statistics on the number of times these words were found when Scooter searched the Web.

the	187,110,494	on	26,600,315
of	106,688,578	www	25,102,096
and	94,539,071	that	24,821,167
to	86,630,491	edu	24,748,535
a	84,912,996	I	23,519,187
in	60,667,757	with	21,373,910
html	57,888,283	be	20,748,021
for	40,233,791	it	20,725,688
is	39,247,605	you	20,280,396
http	36,951,231	by	20,164,811
i	29,335,603	this	20,164,692
s	27,981,291	com	19,243,957
The	27,587,905	or	19,195,072

A	18,823,883	he	6,570,889
are	18,587,420	index	6,517,709
as	17,985,117	more	6,186,273
from	16,660,150	ftp	5,999,348
at	15,730,540	ac	5,985,735
not	12,792,129	about	5,909,982
an	12,575,721	ime	5,848,868
de	12,449,037	get	5,745,853
will	11,186,495	there	5,548,499
have	11,129,882	their	5,490,245
was	10,172,737	data	5,447,669
all	10,079,535	up	5,444,058
if	10,032,474	system	5,384,744
gif	9,745,897	university	5,366,807
can	9,583,532	what	5,326,148
we	8,438,765	In	5,305,240
information	8,387,273	use	5,279,828
your	8,355,370	do	5,170,413
htm	7,975,424	also	5,130,743
which	7,940,840	file	5,077,087
one	7,895,192	name	5,040,272
no	7,749,630	his	4,994,192
may	7,543,923	when	4,979,931
but	7,323,708	my	4,969,812
new	7,258,653	any	4,965,042
page	7,251,462	University	4,950,212
This	7,197,729	so	4,947,789
net	7,074,165	ca	4,873,859
has	7,033,312	some	4,717,207
other	6,935,396	M	4,712,826
they	6,685,830	these	4,692,658
home	6,677,299	out	4,631,563

It	4,577,481	state	3,714,309
f	4,568,650	Page	3,697,243
txt	4,460,882	end	3,678,548
h	4,445,738	people	3,676,633
line	4,440,164	software	3,662,618
re	4,403,983	than	3,653,944
who	4,383,275	how	3,642,822
uk	4,273,649	see	3,598,382
only	4,239,479	computer	3,584,409
been	4,238,436	systems	3,574,551
us	4,204,915	sep	3,567,510
If	4,202,751	gov	3,557,274
mail	4,137,470	like	3,499,563
first	4,062,013	should	3,475,936
list	4,060,882	pub	3,471,994
bin	4,024,537	Sep	3,424,980
la	4,014,189	then	3,399,586
N	3,983,736	such	3,374,458
our	3,983,534	date	3,365,955
research	3,940,602	used	3,347,848
would	3,909,458	world	3,337,450
its	3,908,959	info	3,313,984
cgi	3,898,056	had	3,298,845
internet	3,835,640	them	3,294,616
en	3,830,024	To	3,280,423
were	3,826,529	work	3,250,401
number	3,812,108	web	3,223,347
program	3,785,537	each	3,213,159
me	3,785,019	last	3,190,316
news	3,776,333	For	3,183,321
X	3,748,112	services	3,176,722
into	3,736,584	public	3,160,517
two	3,717,419	Home	3,151,378

available	3,135,118	au	2,647,999
Internet	3,089,082	many	2,639,812
back	3,065,178	help	2,628,825
cs	3,052,839	where	2,608,445
mailto	3,030,130	network	2,593,650
most	3,017,837	Re	2,590,620
You	3,011,697	user	2,548,948
over	2,956,113	subject	2,547,293
here	2,937,449	go	2,546,426
org	2,891,100	support	2,526,340
We	2,883,930	after	2,524,264
service	2,857,026	files	2,514,378
server	2,853,357	access	2,507,814
May	2,837,844	images	2,483,995
type	2,834,235	HTML	2,475,892
through	2,812,440	aug	2,469,466
now	2,807,680	error	2,459,427
New	2,803,060	HTTP	2,440,379
using	2,792,081	part	2,437,773
year	2,776,040	students	2,435,214
jp	2,772,009	die	2,432,619
text	2,766,400	return	2,425,078
co	2,764,429	her	2,421,697
well	2,749,112	center	2,420,409
next	2,741,638	general	2,414,397
k	2,725,150	under	2,406,425
Information	2,718,362	science	2,402,949
group	2,699,923	message	2,385,688
just	2,687,398	GET	2,373,713
set	2,676,095	zip	2,372,026
must	2,667,394	address	2,342,141
make	2,657,048	library	2,335,294

A

From	2,327,404	said	2,059,226
order	2,323,251	those	2,058,644
Aug	2,321,076	search	2,056,854
high	2,318,828	And	2,036,721
inc	2,298,671	day	2,031,381
gopher	2,295,118	know	2,026,031
very	2,288,027	Jul	2,024,082
development	2,273,536	All	2,017,719
business	2,250,677	Web	2,010,297
she	2,249,706	des	2,009,035
technology	2,246,224	following	2,008,611
pages	2,245,339	course	2,008,555
version	2,204,165	please	2,008,194
und	2,199,077	What	2,008,062
No	2,192,585	area	2,001,458
man	2,177,074	control	1,998,493
way	2,175,313	am	1,995,868
section	2,174,671	years	1,988,061
department	2,151,453	management	1,984,467
THE	2,148,242	both	1,983,000
national	2,147,623	id	1,978,495
jpg	2,139,130	contact	1,972,093
OF	2,136,512	same	1,956,166
jul	2,134,755	need	1,956,085
local	2,131,332	because	1,950,369
TXT	2,130,529	could	1,947,662
between	2,119,920	music	1,945,924
don	2,113,873	education	1,944,220
school	2,096,486	before	1,938,247
form	2,086,593	jun	1,927,597
good	2,068,895	site	1,926,285
fax	2,063,719	project	1,912,181

Date	1,902,622	level	1,731,092
WWW	1,901,577	shall	1,717,505
international	1,901,102	take	1,716,238
directory	1,898,872	alt	1,712,892
based	1,897,649	right	1,712,475
windows	1,896,723	State	1,705,192
users	1,894,688	top	1,703,514
send	1,885,046	Error	1,698,924
mit	1,881,008	find	1,698,351
code	1,873,878	want	1,688,423
three	1,855,076	student	1,687,518
design	1,853,859	le	1,686,989
made	1,853,235	Computer	1,686,772
current	1,853,040	email	1,682,707
include	1,852,407	life	1,681,856
call	1,839,671	sun	1,680,909
There	1,826,423	while	1,678,673
Inc	1,825,831	Department	1,675,584
being	1,822,247	resources	1,669,875
does	1,821,929	jan	1,666,999
Research	1,820,381	description	1,657,765
Jun	1,809,991	free	1,655,399
per	1,808,434	document	1,649,637
him	1,795,259	much	1,648,615
city	1,795,093	class	1,646,258
long	1,787,440	mar	1,643,369
Center	1,783,183	example	1,633,411
programs	1,776,216	value	1,627,719
office	1,753,022	copyright	1,625,831
even	1,744,484	source	1,619,878
title	1,742,127	phone	1,619,643
image	1,741,103	point	1,616,661

A

college	1,614,050	fr	1,521,287
including	1,612,951	provide	1,513,030
command	1,612,948	law	1,512,222
Science	1,611,163	special	1,510,613
archive	1,607,391	without	1,508,620
another	1,603,680	pc	1,508,081
report	1,600,625	comp	1,505,684
start	1,598,008	since	1,503,104
company	1,590,702	Mar	1,502,464
john	1,585,750	dr	1,498,744
total	1,581,380	case	1,498,719
apr	1,578,278	own	1,497,165
down	1,574,360	feb	1,496,658
open	1,573,978	health	1,492,972
non	1,572,375	change	1,491,925
full	1,567,935	National	1,488,038
process	1,563,481	Index	1,486,257
products	1,561,145	ch	1,484,234
off	1,557,428	size	1,484,070
during	1,557,002	different	1,481,195
engineering	1,556,538	main	1,478,989
space	1,555,304	Windows	1,478,532
img	1,555,118	uni	1,477,359
Last	1,553,648	World	1,475,816
unix	1,553,001	Apr	1,472,059
cc	1,552,904	dec	1,471,387
Jan	1,547,490	comments	1,462,822
within	1,538,985	read	1,458,257
american	1,536,707	author	1,457,608
place	1,533,901	table	1,455,565
AND	1,530,782	AE	1,454,316
note	1,521,716	System	1,453,507

applications	1,447,638	IN	1,366,606
small	1,447,084	When	1,366,383
government	1,446,516	un	1,365,912
But	1,434,347	American	1,364,589
test	1,429,064	ibm	1,363,115
ms	1,427,253	old	1,348,992
mac	1,426,298	etc	1,344,943
application	1,426,040	guide	1,344,926
states	1,416,272	links	1,339,680
Systems	1,413,275	analysis	1,338,264
map	1,412,989	IMG	1,337,879
best	1,412,400	rw	1,333,146
format	1,409,751	usa	1,332,117
As	1,409,696	language	1,331,578
art	1,406,077	bytes	1,329,462
history	1,404,682	previous	1,329,177
Feb	1,404,189	These	1,327,079
defined	1,404,065	water	1,324,025
real	1,403,619	que	1,323,902
field	1,401,291	nasa	1,323,787
box	1,401,106	Services	1,321,644
second	1,400,949	however	1,320,462
On	1,398,560	database	1,320,142
John	1,391,612	think	1,312,312
power	1,388,433	Return	1,310,229
They	1,387,582	still	1,308,738
staff	1,384,291	product	1,306,622
book	1,383,217	contents	1,305,972
Subject	1,381,881	standard	1,305,839
key	1,375,329	found	1,301,474
CA	1,368,177	great	1,296,446
cd	1,368,085	Software	1,295,499

problems	1,294,492	press	1,224,911
add	1,292,540	Library	1,216,383
study	1,289,615	function	1,211,077
welcome	1,286,645	model	1,208,981
oct	1,285,138	Name	1,206,619
show	1,284,489	al	1,204,993
problem	1,281,328	major	1,204,154
faq	1,280,524	related	1,203,179
received	1,280,477	house	1,195,742
An	1,275,933	run	1,195,147
How	1,274,096	Data	1,190,468
graphics	1,273,643	College	1,188,901
ps	1,272,641	come	1,184,567
online	1,270,649	washington	1,184,564
community	1,269,187	Oct	1,181,468
les	1,268,614	look	1,179,967
every	1,262,788	several	1,179,204
US	1,260,723	technical	1,178,538
Dr	1,258,963	link	1,177,615
wide	1,256,446	misc	1,173,280
object	1,250,656	dir	1,170,739
el	1,248,365	little	1,170,256
van	1,246,708	too	1,165,297
questions	1,240,426	body	1,163,062
electronic	1,238,868	united	1,162,692
large	1,237,851	Copyright	1,158,402
human	1,237,850	menu	1,154,957
members	1,236,591	performance	1,152,760
did	1,234,219	issues	1,147,305
required	1,231,470	USA	1,147,167
around	1,230,999	courses	1,145,507
International	1,225,237	studies	1,144,065

environment	1,143,306	reference	1,077,699
english	1,139,930	working	1,074,646
School	1,138,477	price	1,073,334
called	1,138,347	air	1,071,745
possible	1,138,158	security	1,071,699
One	1,138,059	conference	1,070,949
person	1,137,532	General	1,069,096
CD	1,125,232	let	1,063,924
sites	1,123,290	video	1,062,693
given	1,121,027	left	1,061,587
Fax	1,120,794	tue	1,061,188
single	1,118,798	david	1,058,872
county	1,118,701	institute	1,058,704
Back	1,115,115	say	1,058,499
root	1,113,263	game	1,057,623
board	1,112,797	might	1,056,353
via	1,111,454	provides	1,055,527
above	1,107,459	Group	1,054,968
times	1,106,903	important	1,054,851
doc	1,104,497	article	1,053,926
Other	1,097,580	media	1,053,789
Sun	1,097,542	why	1,050,647
mr	1,095,864	family	1,047,901
personal	1,095,135	@	1,045,654
den	1,093,948	interface	1,045,127
faculty	1,092,785	room	1,043,931
Technology	1,092,428	york	1,043,376
homepage	1,090,064	Engineering	1,042,230
north	1,083,457	mon	1,039,473
click	1,081,539	del	1,037,456
things	1,081,002	few	1,036,419
paper	1,080,321	nov	1,034,595

A

training	1,033,939	Next	1,002,754
status	1,033,831	request	1,001,391
pm	1,033,480	wed	1,000,372
Network	1,033,115	complete	1,000,316
bit	1,032,017	stack	999,330
hours	1,030,857	est	998,934
Server	1,030,454	City	997,248
Service	1,030,341	give	996,974
Program	1,027,911	areas	996,324
PC	1,026,925	projects	994,508
Office	1,026,753	july	987,692
journal	1,026,545	experience	987,574
United	1,024,809	News	984,175
cost	1,021,736	social	983,004
word	1,021,650	san	981,534
St	1,020,310	quality	980,978
rights	1,020,256	specific	980,109
Please	1,017,914	thu	979,652
view	1,013,394	common	979,407
fri	1,013,115	books	979,257
put	1,012,979	canada	976,941
society	1,012,840	again	975,251
week	1,011,783	Wed	973,725
med	1,009,189	june	972,347
results	1,006,671	Institute	972,309
country	1,006,668	Fri	971,695
digital	1,006,462	communications	969,536
Education	1,006,218	better	969,298
september	1,005,158	action	967,298
four	1,005,039	series	962,920
List	1,003,494	includes	962,297
provided	1,003,343	either	961,204

See	960,012	groups	927,457
review	959,188	going	927,281
white	956,101	committee	925,742
never	955,903	means	924,227
tools	955,790	present	924,126
lib	955,175	something	923,599
future	951,462	June	922,520
days	950,476	august	920,679
interest	950,461	linux	920,414
upon	949,412	Phone	919,135
Dec	946,252	York	917,798
children	943,932	member	916,039
Thu	941,869	plan	914,472
got	940,711	california	914,339
requirements	940,659	various	914,096
low	939,351	My	912,476
States	938,517	once	912,341
below	938,218	yes	912,083
David	937,194	organization	911,212
team	937,102	south	910,952
September	936,589	created	910,454
really	936,303	medical	909,057
less	935,247	lines	907,329
Nov	935,005	usr	906,990
July	932,699	god	905,670
write	930,918	Mail	905,262
women	930,571	output	904,695
physics	930,399	Management	904,613
check	930,015	policy	904,395
Business	928,986	sound	904,232
modified	928,899	activities	903,694
Mon	927,653	computing	903,530

At	902,371	copy	872,900
act	901,370	August	872,247
Tue	900,626	print	871,817
default	898,646	term	871,411
industry	898,556	Your	869,054
documents	896,814	County	866,564
changes	894,618	lcast	864,050
done	893,553	against	863,864
until	893,540	job	863,834
street	891,917	card	862,905
range	890,934	Canada	862,808
building	890,477	Mr	861,824
Description	889,337	By	860,258
input	885,686	written	859,638
basic	885,023	market	859,568
machine	884,707	energy	858,975
always	883,698	display	857,748
post	883,488	president	856,809
meeting	883,015	care	856,708
federal	881,267	plus	854,387
mil	879,722	association	854,227
structure	878,634	dtd	851,951
docs	878,483	Some	851,393
others	878,469	head	850,449
That	877,923	notes	850,445
features	877,741	west	845,883
location	877,271	hqx	845,724
issue	876,519	math	845,301
sent	876,282	thinks	844,982
mode	875,414	processing	842,184
host	873,999	sat	841,416
updated	873,049	today	841,390

black	840,412		question	814,078
equipment	839,829		record	814,030
California	839,732		games	813,294
interpreter	838,759		item	812,601
So	837,107		able	812,243
color	836,168		short	811,821
IBM	836,134		With	811,617
mark	836,017		Stack	811,210
events	834,354		further	811,062
gmt	834,262		yet	810,123
os	834,203		introduction	808,483
men	832,966		position	807,324
environmental	831,440		rate	805,854
GMT	830,395		needs	805,495
arts	828,798		disk	802,784
San	828,379		america	802,277
director	827,257		memory	801,890
na	826,797		Time	801,357
dos	824,485		FOR	801,006
base	824,256		nbsp	799,312
additional	823,992		hand	798,540
materials	823,437		contains	798,050
select	821,762		av	796,947
unit	821,464		First	795,230
reports	820,698		ingrid	793,396
rec	818,391		individual	793,122
messages	818,072		Section	792,978
love	817,844		North	792,970
catalog	815,977		client	792,820
discussion	815,275		stdin	792,584
window	815,252		light	792,558
create	814,492		often	791,787

A

int	790,925	making	771,641
Contact	790,819	computers	771,615
entry	789,503	side	770,980
Number	788,280	EDU	770,198
tex	788,113	chapter	768,129
English	787,537	papers	768,054
programming	787,261	try	767,076
Box	786,959	keep	766,836
far	781,777	string	766,390
communication	781,305	Note	765,863
knowledge	780,684	distribution	765,808
screen	780,312	Development	765,694
fullname	777,917	currently	764,886
radio	776,685	usage	764,803
resource	775,221	material	763,624
big	773,096	begin	761,593
readme	772,887	april	761,026

A Sample of
1,000 Queries

The following is a brief snapshot of the kinds of things that people search for when they use AltaVista Search. This is a sample of 1,000 consecutive queries from the middle of the day on a random day in 1996.

About half of the AltaVista Search queries fell into the following categories:

Description	Approximate Count	Average Words per Query
Products/Product info/Buy and sell	150	2.4
Sex-related	130	2.5
Individuals (ordinary and celebrity)	100	2.0
Non-English queries	100	1.4
Places/Travel	75	1.8
News (world events news/locate past article)	25	3.7
Miscellaneous queries	420	2.1

Miscellaneous Queries

The miscellaneous queries included searches for the following subjects (capitalization and spelling have been kept as entered):

- Education, including
  - diploma factory
  - Museum of Science and Industry Chicago
  - Wheaton college
  - chemistry uc san diego
  - multicultural education
  - student WWW magazine university
  - university of pittsburg
  - "Drew University"
- EDUCATION REFORM CAREER ACADEMIES

- Elderly/Aging, including
  - premature senility
  - Charlestown retirement community
- Catonsville Maryland
- Environment
  - ozone ions
  - Clean-Water-Act and NPDES
- Family
  - children chorus preschool
  - High AND School AND Iowa
  - family history quebec
  - tennesse geneology o'dell
- Government, including
  - Federal Election Commission
  - United States Department of Transporatation
  - "United Nations" AND grants AND language
  - Social+Security+Administration
- Handicap Access, including
  - computers and the visually impaired
  - epileptics and computers
- History/General, including
  - serfdom in Russia
- History/Military, including
  - U-boats
  - Yankee Air Force
  - army and helicopter

B

- "pictures of military arms"
- Hobbies, including
    - birmingham uk painting courses
    - California "Gardening"
    - yarn suppliers
- Investment, including
    - financial management construction property research
- Job/Employment Opportunities, including
    - occupational titles
    - information on how to start an importing business
    - american association for the advancement of science science
    - "help wanted Field Engineer"
    - employment "finance"
    - contract recruitment
    - "employment testing"
    - "American Red Cross" employment
    - resume and writing
    - Cruiseline Employment
- Literature, including
    - american indian songs and literature
    - books authors
    - mythological AND criticism
    - neuromancer gibson
- Medical Care/Medical Conditions/Medicine, including
    - Blue Cross Insurance
    - dutch health care

- medical malpractice
- cardiology
- Health care rationing
- Attention Deficit Disability
- autism
- medical encyclopedia online
- pelvic varicosities
- congenital hearing defect
- aromatheraphy
- how to treat bacillus infections in surgical patients
- houston chronicle ebola virus
- centers for disease control injury prevention
- county health statistics
- elm and bark and beetle
- EPIDEMIOLOGY AND CHLORINE
- treating varroa jacobsoni mite
- proanthocyanidins

- Metal, including
  - variable AND length AND subnetting
  - "Light Emitting Diodes" AND Spectroscopy
  - Thevenin
- Movies, including
  - "muppet treasure"
  - mortal kombat movie
  - Monkeys"

- Music, including
    - "billy white trio"
    - debussy and (stravinsky or ravel) and music and not concert and not
- Pets and Animals, including
    - Rottweiler "picture"
    - cats & (claw | declaw)
    - Bats
    - blackbird
    - dinosaur +egg
    - appaloosa
- Recording, including
    - Venice AND music AND baroque
    - +irish +music +francisco
    - Karaoke
    - banjo
- Religion, including
    - buddism
    - "Online Bible" "ONLINE BIBLE"
- Science, including
    - american association for the advancement of science
- Sports, including
    - chicago cubs schedule
    - pirates
    - packers
    - torrey pines press insulin -golf -inn -stock

- Baseball mit
- mba AND rank
- Video Games, including
  - Nintendo Rygar
- Weather, including
  - Old Farmer's Almanac

B

C

Frequency of Words Used in AltaVista Search Queries

Kathy Richardson of Digital took a snapshot of AltaVista Search use on a random day to determine what people were searching for. Most of the words most frequently used in queries are the query commands (like *and* or *not*), although *software* and *windows* are among the most frequently used words. This is a brief list of some of the most commonly typed words in order of occurrence:

139,902	and	14,995	NEAR
86,158	AND	11,218	the
22,330	or	9,798	jpg
21,903	of	9,774	software
21,717	pictures	9,090	windows
20,902	OR	7,051	in
16,094	near	6,989	NOT

On the other hand, these words represent a relatively small percentage of the total number of query words. The only query words that are used in over 1% of the queries are query commands (*AND/and/OR/or*). Out of 1.8 million queries sampled, there is a tremendous diversity in the words that AltaVista Search users searched for, as shown by the percentages listed below.

A listing of 3.5% for the word *and* means that of the 1.8 million queries sampled, *and* was used in a query 3.5% of the time.

3.50%	and
2.15%	AND
0.59%	or
0.58%	of
0.54%	pictures
0.52%	OR
0.40%	near
0.37%	NEAR
0.28%	the
0.24%	jpg

0.24%	software
0.23%	windows
0.18%	in
0.17%	NOT

The total number of words used in the queries sampled was 3,999,449 in 1,857,630 queries, or an average of 2.2 words per query. On the day when this sample was taken, 282,631 unique words were used.

In addition, here are a few other interesting facts about the words people use in their searches:

- The top 250 words account for only 25% of the query words used.

- The top 2,500 words account for only 50% of the query words used.

- The top 17,500 words account for only 75% of the query words used.

- The top 70,000 words account for about 90% of the query words used.

C

A

A to Z search reference, 107-214
   conventions, 111
   how to use, 110-111
Abstracts (and Web site searches), 93-94
Acquaintances, search for, 111
Advanced Search, 37-57
   by date, 48-50
   example of, 52-55
   Results Ranking, 50-51
   vs. Simple Search, 55-57
   of Usenet newsgroups, 76-81
   using operators, 42-48
   when to use, 39
Advanced Search Form, 41-52
Advanced Search page, 39-41
African philosophy, search for, 112
African-American history and literature, 112
Alpha computer systems, 223, 226-228
AltaVista CyberCast, 235
AltaVista Internet Software, 235
AltaVista Search
   ease of use, 4
   frequency of words sought, 263-265
   genesis of, 216
   home page, 10-18
   revolution, 8
   scope of, 3
   speed of, 3-4, 222
   as the standard, 7-8
AltaVista story, 215-237
   building the prototype, 228-229
   the continuing revolution, 237
   Digital's research, 217-218
   extending success, 236-237
   genesis, 216
   internal pilot, 232-234
   the launch, 234-235
   pioneering the Internet, 218-228
   the pitch, 230-234
   product naming, 232-233
Anchor, Simple Search by, 32
AND operator, 42-43, 79
Annual reports, search for, 112-113
Anonymity, search for, 114
Applet, Simple Search by, 33
Art (images), search for, 114-115, 126
Asterisk (*) in wildcard searches, 28-29
Astronomy, search for, 115

B

Baby names, search for, 179
Baseball cards, search for, 116
Basketball, search for, 116-117
Beekeeping, search for, 117-118
Bicycling, search for, 118
Binary option, 68
Biochemistry, search for, 118
Birds, search for, 46
Blind, search for, 119
Bookmarking a search, 21
Brewing, search for, 119-120
Business, search for, 120-121
Business marketing plan search, 52-55

INDEX

C

Canine, search for, 121-122
Caning furniture, search for, 122
Capitalization, 26-27
Cappuccino, search for, 138
Cars, search for, 122-123
CD-ROM development, search for, 123-124
Character substitutions (special characters), 27-28
Chemistry, search for, 124
Chess, search for, 124-125
Child development, search for, 125-126
Clip art, search for, 126
Coconut oil, search for, 127
Colleges, search for, 127-128
Combining Simple Search elements, 35-36
Comic books, search for, 128-129
Common words on the World Wide Web, 239-254
Compact Form, 16-17
Company annual reports, search for, 112-113
Computers, search for, 129, 151-152
Content providers' AltaVista guide, 84-103
Contests, search for, 129-130
Cooking, search for, 130-131
Copyright issues, search for, 131-132
Counting results, 51-52
Cycling, search for, 118

D

Dance, search for, 132-133
Dance school, search for, 133

Database vs. index, 223-224

Database vs. index, 223-224
Dates, using in searches, 48-50, 94
Daycare, search for, 133
Diet/lowfat reference, search for, 134
Digital's Palo Alto Lab, 218-220
Digital's research, 217-218
Directories, Internet, 6-7
Dogs, search for, 121-122
Domain, Simple Search by, 32-33
Donations, search for, 134
Drug side effects, search for, 195
Drums, search for, 135

E

Ease of use of AltaVista Search, 4
Education, search for, 127-128, 136
Electrical repair, search for, 154
Emergency planning, search for, 136-137
Empire State Building, search for, 137
Employee relations, search for, 139
Environment, search for, 137
Ergonomics, search for, 137-138
Espresso, search for, 138
Excluding words/phrases (Simple Search), 34-35
Exercise, search for, 139-140
Expressions, grouping (Advanced Search), 45-47

F

Face-making, search for, 165
Fast food, search for, 140
Fires, search for, 142-143

Firewalls, 233
Fish, search for, 140-141
Flaherty, Paul, 220
Flying, search for, 141
Footers, 12, 69
Foreign language and culture, search for, 142
Forest fires, search for, 142-143
Forestry, search for, 143
Friends, search for, 111, 182
Frisbee, search for, 143
From, newsgroup search by, 69
Full text search, 220
Fuller, Sam, 217

G

Gambling, search for, 144
Games, search for, 144-147
Gardening, searches for, 50, 146-147
Genealogy, search for, 148
Geography, search for, 148-149
Getting started, search for, 149-150
Government, search for, 150-151
Grouping operators and expressions, 45-47

H

Hand-held computers, search for, 151-152
Health, search for, 152
Herbs, search for, 152-153
Hexadecimal, search for, 153
Hiccups, search for, 153
Hit-or-miss approach, 22

Home page (AltaVista Search), 10-17
Home page (yours)
    including AltaVista Search in, 35
    making AltaVista Search your home page, 17-18
Home repair—electrical, search for, 154
Home repair—plumbing, search for, 154-155
Homework, search for, 155
Horse, search for, 155-156
Host, Simple Search by, 32
Hovercraft, search for, 156
HTML document titles (Web site searches), 92-93
Humor, search for, 156-157

I

Ice cores, search for, 157
Igloo, search for, 158
Image, Simple Search by, 33
Images (art), search for, 114-115, 126
Index vs. database, 223-224
Indexing software, how it works, 224-225
Indoor plants, search for, 158-159
Internet
    history of, 4-5
    piping information into, 230
Internet directories, 6-7
Internet pioneering, 218-228
    building a showcase, 220-221
    database vs. index, 223-224
    making it happen, 225-226
Intranets, 233
Investments, search for, 159-160

J

Jargon, search for, 160
Jazz, search for, 160-161
Jobs, search for, 161-162

K

Keys/locks, search for, 163
Keywords
    newsgroup search by, 71
    Web site search by, 94-96
Kid's story, search for, 164
Kites, search for, 164
Knitting, search for, 164-165

L

Lang, Ilene, 235
Language, search for, 165-166
Language and culture, search for, 142
Lesson plans, search for, 166-167
Librarians, search for, 167
Lighthouses, search for, 167-168
Link, Simple Search by, 32
Local option, 67-68
Logan's Run, search for, 168
Lowfat reference, search for, 134
Lyrics, search for, 168-169

M

Magic, search for, 174
Marketing research, search for,
    169-170

Mars, search for, 170
Medical information, search for,
    170-173
Medical topics—general, search for,
    170-171
Medical topics—rare, search for,
    171-172
Medical topics—specific, search for,
    172
Meetings, search for, 173-174
Metal, search for, 174
Money, search for, 175
Monier, Louis, 220-222, 226, 228-231
Most common words on the World
    Wide Web, 239-254
Movies, search for, 175-176
Multimedia files (Web site), 90
Music, search for, 176-178

N

Names for baby, search for, 179
Naming of AltaVista products, 232-233
Naming your publication or Web site,
    178-179
NASCAR races, search for, 179
Native Americans, search for, 46-47
Natural history, search for, 179-180
Navigation bar, 11-13
Navigation choices, 12-13
NEAR operator, 42-44, 79
Network news. *See* Usenet newsgroups
New age, search for, 180
News archives, search for, 180-181
Newsgroups. *See* Usenet newsgroup
    searches; Usenet newsgroups
NOT operator, 42-43, 79

Old friends, search for, 182
Operators
    in Advanced vs. Simple Search, 55-56
    grouping in Advanced Search, 45-47
    using in Advanced Search, 42-48, 79
Opinions, search for, 181
OR operator, 42-43, 79
Outdoor activities, search for, 182-183

P

Palmer, Bob, 235
Paquette, Joella, 220
Parentheses, using in Advanced Search, 45
Parenting, search for, 183-184
Peanut butter, search for, 184
People, search for, 111, 182
Personality profile, search for, 184-185
Photography, search for, 185-186
Phrases (in Simple Search)
    excluding, 34-35
    requiring, 34
    using, 25
Piping information into the Internet, 230
Plants (indoor), search for, 158-159
Plumbing, search for, 154-155
Poetry, search for, 186
Political topics, search for, 187
Publication, naming, 178-179
Publishers, search for, 188
Punctuation

    in Advanced vs. Simple Search, 57
    using in Simple Search, 26

Q

Queries, snapshot sample of, 255-261
Question, entering Simple Search as, 25
Quilting and quilts, search for, 189
Quotations, search for, 189-190

R

Radio, search for, 190-191
RAID system, 222
Ranking Results (Advanced Search), 50-51
Ranking of Web sites, 87-89
Rare words, using in Simple Search, 23-24
Real estate, search for, 192
Recipes, search for, 134, 192
Reid, Brian, 220, 234
Replies to newsgroup postings, finding, 73
Requiring words/phrases (Simple Search), 34
Research, search for, 191, 193
Results
    counts of, 51-52
    newsgroup search, 65-69
    ranking Advanced Search, 50-51
    saving Simple Search, 20-21
Roller coaster, search for, 193
Rules, Advanced vs. Simple Search, 56

S

Saving Simple Search results, 20-21
Scanner, search for, 194
Scooter (AltaVista Search spider),
    85-86, 221-223, 228-229
Scope of AltaVista Search, 3
Search engines, 7
Search Form, 12
    Advanced, 41-52
    Simple, 13-14
Search reference (A to Z), 107-214
Shareware, search for, 195
Shortcut equivalents for operators,
    using, 42
Side effects, search for, 195
Simple Search, 18-36
    vs. Advanced Search, 55-57
    combining elements in, 35-36
    excluding words/phrases, 34-35
    hit-or-miss approach, 22
    requiring words/phrases, 34
    saving results, 20-21
    with standard output, 19-20
    by structural elements, 30-33
    using all words, 24-25
    using capitalization, 26-27
    using phrases, 25
    using punctuation and spaces, 26
    using a question, 25
    using rare words, 23-24
    using wildcards, 28-29
Simple Search Form, 13-14
Sites, Dick, 227
Skating, search for, 195-196
Software, search for, 196
Souvenir, search for, 196-197
Spaces, using in Simple Search, 26

Special character substitutions, 27-28
Speed of AltaVista Search, 3-4, 222
Spelling, searching for most used, 197
Sports, search for, 197-198
Standard Form, 14-16
Standard output, Simple Search with,
    19-20
Standard Results, 15
Standards, search for, 198-199
Steffora, Philip, 221
Strecker, Bill, 217
Structural elements
    newsgroup search by, 69-71
    Simple Search by, 30-33
Stuart, Stephen, 225-226, 230
Subject, newsgroup search by, 70
Substance abuse, search for, 199
Summary, newsgroup search by, 71
Supnik, Bob, 226
Support groups, search for, 199-200

T

Taxes, search for, 201
Tests, search for, 200-201
Text, Simple Search by, 31
Text-Only page, 12
Tip (home page), 11
Title, Simple Search by, 31
Tools, search for, 203
Trademarks, search for, 201
Travel, search for, 202-203
Trewitt, Glenn, 225-226
Trivia, search for, 203-204
Troubleshooting (Advanced Search),
    47-48
Tunnels, 233

U

UFO, search for, 207
Universities, search for, 127-128
Urban legends, search for, 207-208
URL Simple Search, 32
URL (Web address), 15
Usenet newsgroup searches, 59-81
    Advanced Search, 76-81
    excluding articles from AltaVista
      Search, 104-105
    how AltaVista Search finds
      articles, 104
    by newsgroup, 71
    results, 65-69
    structural elements, 69-71
Usenet newsgroups, 6
    categories of, 71-72
    finding replies to postings, 73
    keeping postings from indexers,
      75-76

V

Vacation rentals, search for, 204
Vegetable gardening, search for, 50
Vegetarian potluck dinner search, 38
Volcano, search for, 205

W

Warren, Annie, 226, 234
Weather, search for, 205-206
Web site searches
    and abstracts, 93-94
    and dates, 94
    excluding your site from, 96-98
    and HTML document titles, 92-93
    and keywords, 94-96
    using AltaVista Search for, 105
Web sites
    controlling how AltaVista Search
      indexes, 91
    designing, 98-99
    fixing broken links, 102
    how AltaVista Search finds, 85-86
    how AltaVista Search indexes,
      86-87
    how AltaVista Search ranks,
      87-89
    inventory of links, 100-101
    keeping information private, 100
    keeping up with links, 101
    naming, 178-179
    overall inventory, 102-103
    submitting, 86
    what AltaVista Search does not
      index, 89-91
Web statistics, search for, 206
Webmasters
    AltaVista guide, 84-103
    useful techniques for, 100-103
Wildcards, using in Simple Search,
    28-29
Women's issues, search for, 206
Words
    excluding in Simple Search,
      34-35
    frequency of in AltaVista
      Searches, 263-265
    most common on the World Wide
      Web, 239-254
    requiring in Simple Search, 34
Work from home, search for, 208-209

World almanac, search for, 209
World Wide Web. *See also* Web site
   searches; Web sites
     history of, 5-6
     most common words on, 239-254

X

Xena Warrior Princess, search for, 209
Xylography, search for, 210

Y

Yachting, search for, 210
Yellow pages, search for, 211

Z

Zimbabwe, search for, 211-212
Zine, search for, 212-213
Zip codes, search for, 213
Zodiac, search for, 213-214
Zoo, search for, 214

The Books to Use When There's

Save Time and Get
the Information You
Need with this Critically
Acclaimed Series from
Osborne/McGraw-Hill.

**The Internet
for Busy People**
by Christian Crumlish
$22.95 USA
ISBN: 0-07-882108-8

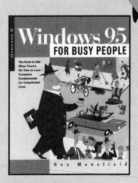

**Windows 95
for Busy People**
by Ron Mansfield
$22.95 USA
ISBN: 0-07-882110-X

**Word for Windows 95
for Busy People**
by Christian Crumlish
$22.95 USA
ISBN: 0-07-882109-6

**Excel for Windows 95
for Busy People**
by Ron Mansfield
$22.95 USA
ISBN: 0-07-882111-8

To Order, Call 1-800-262-4729

No Time to Lose!

Computer Fundamentals for Complicated Lives

Whether you set aside an evening or lunch hour, reach for a **BUSY PEOPLE** guide and you're guaranteed to save time! Organized for a quick orientation to the most popular computer hardware and software applications, each **BUSY PEOPLE** title offers exceptional timesaving features and has the right blend of vital skills and handy shortcuts that you must know to get a job done quickly and accurately. Full-color text makes the going easy and fun.

Written by a busy person (like you!) with a skeptic's view of computing, these opinionated, well-organized, and authoritative books are all you'll need to master the important ins and outs of the best-selling software releases, hardware, and the Internet—without wasting your precious hours!

Access for Windows 95 for Busy People
by Alan Neibauer
$22.95 USA
ISBN: 0-07-882112-6

PCs for Busy People
by David Einstein
$22.95 USA
ISBN: 0-07-882210-6

PowerPoint for Windows 95 for Busy People
by Ron Mansfield
$22.95 USA
ISBN: 0-07-882204-1

Web Publishing with Netscape for Busy People
by Christian Crumlish and Malcolm Humes
$22.95 USA
ISBN: 0-07-882144-4

http:// www.osborne.com

OSBORNE

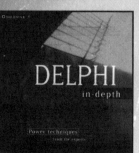

DIGITAL DESIGN
FOR THE
21ST CENTURY

You can count on Osborne/McGraw-Hill and its expert authors to bring you the inside scoop on digital design, production, and the best-selling graphics software.

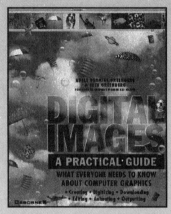

Digital Images: A Practical Guide
by Adele Droblas Greenberg
and Seth Greenberg
$26.95 U.S.A.
ISBN 0-07-882113-4

Scanning the Professional Way
by Sybil Ihrig and Emil Ihrig
$21.95 U.S.A.
ISBN 0-07-882145-2

Preparing Digital Images for Print
by Sybil Ihrig and Emil Ihrig
$21.95 U.S.A.
ISBN 0-07-882146-0

**Fundamental Photoshop:
A Complete Introduction,
Second Edition**
by Adele Droblas Greenberg
and Seth Greenberg
$29.95 U.S.A.
ISBN 0-07-882093-6

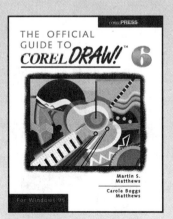

**The Official Guide to
CorelDRAW!™6 for Windows 95**
by Martin S. Matthews and Carole Boggs Matthews
$34.95 U.S.A.
ISBN 0-07-882168-1

**The Official Guide to Corel
PHOTO-PAINT 6**
by David Huss
$34.95 U.S.A.
ISBN 0-07-882207-6

ORDER BOOKS DIRECTLY FROM OSBORNE/McGRAW-HILL

For a complete catalog of Osborne's books, call 510-549-6600 or write to us at 2600 Tenth Street, Berkeley, CA 94710

Call Toll-Free, *24 hours a day, 7 days a week, in the U.S.A.*
U.S.A.: 1-800-262-4729   **Canada: 1-800-565-5758**

Mail *in the U.S.A. to:*   **Canada**
McGraw-Hill, Inc.   McGraw-Hill Ryerson
Customer Service Dept.   Customer Service
P.O. Box 182607   300 Water Street
Columbus, OH 43218-2607   Whitby, Ontario L1N 9B6

Fax *in the U.S.A. to:*   **Canada**
1-614-759-3644   1-800-463-5885
                                   Canada
                                   orders@mcgrawhill.ca

SHIP TO:

Name _____

Company _____

Address _____

City / State / Zip _____

Daytime Telephone *(We'll contact you if there's a question about your order.)*

ISBN #	BOOK TITLE	Quantity	Price	Total
0-07-88				
0-07-88				
0-07-88				
0-07-88				
0-07-88				
0-07088				
0-07-88				
0-07-88				
0-07-88				
0-07-88				
0-07-88				
0-07-88				
0-07-88				
0-07-88				

Shipping & Handling Charge from Chart Below		
Subtotal		
Please Add Applicable State & Local Sales Tax		
TOTAL		

Shipping & Handling Charges

Order Amount	U.S.	Outside U.S.
$15.00 - $24.99	$4.00	$6.00
$25.00 - $49.99	$5.00	$7.00
$50.00 - $74.99	$6.00	$8.00
$75.00 - and up	$7.00	$9.00
$100.00 - and up	$8.00	$10.00

Occasionally we allow other selected companies to use our mailing list. If you would prefer that we not include you in these extra mailings, please check here: ❑

METHOD OF PAYMENT

❑ Check or money order enclosed (payable to Osborne/McGraw-Hill)

❑ AMERICAN EXPRESS   ❑ DISCOVER   ❑ MasterCard   ❑ VISA

Account No. [ ][ ][ ][ ][ ][ ][ ][ ][ ][ ][ ][ ][ ][ ][ ][ ]

Expiration Date _____

Signature _____

In a hurry? Call with your order anytime, day or night, or visit your local bookstore.

Thank you for your order

Code BC640SL